EDUCATING BLACK GIRLS

By Jawanza Kunjufu

Chicago, Illinois

Printed in the United States of America

ISBN #: 1-934155-70-5

ISBN #: 978-1934-155-70-7

Contents

Introduction

I've been an educational consultant and author since 1974, and have written almost 40 books, including *Keeping Black Boys Out of Special Education, Raising Black Boys, Reducing the Black Male Dropout Rate, Understanding Black Male Learning Styles, Changing School Culture for Black Males,* and four volumes of *Countering the Conspiracy to Destroy Black Boys.* In addition, I've written three books for African American men, including *Adam! Where Are You?: Why Most Black Men Don't Go to Church, Developing Strong Black Male Ministries,* and *State of Emergency: We Must Save African American Males.*

I have two grown sons and one grandson. I have dedicated my life to the uplift of African American people.

My remaining books have been coed, but I have never written a book about African American girls and women. As a book publisher, I have sought out women to write them and we have published over 10 books for girls and women. Over the years, hundreds of people, primarily African American women, have asked if I would ever write a book about Black girls. Recently, I was asked to speak to educators in Oakland, California, about the challenges facing African American males. During the question and answer period, an African American woman stood up and asked, "When are you going to talk about African American girls? They're having challenges, too!"

Politely, I said I had been asked to speak about the plight of African American males, but as I flew home that evening I couldn't shake her question. Her passion resonated with me. Her concern about African American girls motivated me to pray about writing such a book, and you now hold the answer to those prayers in your hands. *Educating Black Girls* was written for educators. A companion book for parents, *Raising Black Girls* is forthcoming.

I discovered in my research that all is not well with African American girls. While our boys may be on life support, our girls are in critical condition. We talk about racism in America and

Introduction

throughout the world, but we should not assume that it affects Black boys and Black girls similarly. Though we talk about sexism, we should not assume that White girls and Black girls experience sexism in the same manner. For too long, the plight of Black females has been treated as a stepchild to the plight of Black males and the agenda of White feminists. I am pleased to serve on the task force My Brother's Keeper, President Obama's initiative to support the growth and development of young men of color. This task force should be expanded to include an initiative My Sister's Keeper as well. Young women of color have special challenges and needs, independent of their brothers that would greatly benefit from such national attention and coordination of federal resources.

Throughout this book, we will document the tremendous challenges that African American females are experiencing, particularly in the classroom. Contrary to the cultural deficit model, this book spotlights the best in Black females. We will look at their strengths. In my book, *There's Nothing Wrong with Black Students*, I documented how school districts bring me in to "fix the bad Black children." I believe there is nothing wrong with African American female students, and I prove it in chapter 1, where we set a positive tone for the rest of the book by looking at the best of Black females.

In chapter 2, we will examine trends that demand greater attention from schools, school districts, and policy makers. I can understand why the sister in Oakland had such passion, because all is not well with African American females in the classroom.

In chapter 3, Black Females Speak, I provide a platform for Black females themselves to speak about their own experiences in their own unique ways. We researchers and educators may be talking about them and talking over them, but are we allowing them to talk to us? Most important, are we listening? Black females need to be in the center of this conversation. As I travel the country, I listen carefully to the stories of Black female students, and this chapter documents their voices and concerns.

The educational landscape in America is not the same for all Black females. There's a wide array of school options for Black females. Chapter 4 takes a look at school demographics and how they help shape the educational experiences of these students.

The next chapter on STEM is, for me, one of the most significant in this book. STEM refers to academic programs and careers in science, technology, engineering, and mathematics. Trying to encourage Black females to pursue degrees and careers in math and science has been challenging. We can and must do better to introduce STEM to Black girls and nurture their involvement in these fields.

*His*tory is racist and sexist. Chapter 6, *Her*story, looks at this subject from a much needed female perspective.

Chapter 7 focuses on athletics—gym and sports—as a way to support the physical, mental, psychological, and cognitive development of Black females. From firsthand experience, I know the tremendous benefits athletics can have on academic and personal development.

In chapters 8 and 9, we will look at the educational challenges that Black female students must overcome and how some schools are successfully rising to the challenge.

This book would not be complete without chapter 10, educational options available to Black females after high school. Not all Black females want to attend college after graduation. In this chapter, I will explore the wide range of options that will lead to near immediate job placement after completion. Finally, I will present my closing thoughts in the Epilogue.

Q&A

As you read through the chapters of this book, you'll find that I ask numerous questions. The purpose of these questions is not to shame and blame you, but to get you thinking about how you can help improve the academic performance and overall

Introduction

educational experience of your Black female students. I am confident these questions will stimulate more questions and answers within you, so keep a notebook nearby and write down your honest thoughts. Most important, keep it honest! And by all means, share your thoughts with your colleagues. Encourage them to buy this book, so that everyone is on the same page. Transform your teachers' lounge into a combination war room, research room, and research-based book club room. High performing educators can share strategies and information with one another to improve the classroom experience and ultimately student performance. Keep each other accountable. Let this be the start of a great academic turnaround for Black girls in your school!

Now for our first set of questions. Please read and answer as completely and honestly as you can.

- How significant are African American women teachers to African American girls?
- What is your school doing special for African American girls?
- What percent of your African American female students are proficient or advanced in reading and math?
- Do you, your colleagues, and principal have high expectations of African American female students?
- Do Black girls see themselves in your school's curricula?
- Name the books in your school that were written by Black women writers.
- Do you, your colleagues, and principal understand the variety of Black female learning styles?
- In your school, are Black females made to feel beautiful and intelligent?
- Do you understand the culture of your Black female students?
- Do you like your Black female students?

Lastly, I have a request. I would like for every school in America that has African American female students to post Maya Angelou's poem "Phenomenal Woman" in a prominent, visible place in the school.

I am excited to present this book to you because I believe in Black girls. They are truly phenomenal!

Chapter One: The Best of Black Females

Four-Year-Old Genius Anala Beevers Invited to Join MENSA

Most four-year-olds don't know the name of every state on the map, let alone the capitals. But most kids that age aren't like **Anala Beevers,** a New Orleans-based genius who was recently invited to join MENSA, an international organization for people who score at the 98th percentile or higher on a standardized, supervised IQ or other approved intelligence test. Beevers—who never leaves home without her map of the United States, which is said to be her favorite thing—knew the English alphabet at four months old, and learned numbers in Spanish by the time she was a 1½. Her dad, Landon, who admits his little one is smarter than both of her parents, said in a recent interview, "She needs a reality show … She keeps us on our toes."

Zora Ball Becomes Youngest Person to Develop Mobile Game App

One of our top moments of the century is a recent one. **Zora Ball** (pictured), age 7, has the distinction of becoming the youngest person to develop a mobile game app. Ball, a first grader at Harambee Institute of Science and Technology Charter School in Philadelphia, built the game using a programming language called "Bootstrap" that teaches kids age 12 to 16 how to grasp complex math. The prodigious student unveiled her game last December at an expo for the Bootstrap program at the University of Pennsylvania. To prove it wasn't a fluke, Zora was able to break down how her application works right on the spot. The cute little girl's genius aptitude runs in her family: her older brother, **Trace**, was a STEM Scholar of the Year at the Harambee Institute. Makes you want to work a little harder on the job, doesn't it?

Chapter One: The Best of Black Females

Thessalonika Arzu-Embry Graduates College at 14

The exceptional 14-year-old **Thessalonika Arzu-Embry** is preparing to graduate—from college. Like most 14-year-old girls, Thessalonika likes to have fun. She enjoys skating in her Great Lakes neighborhood as well as playing tennis. Yet, while most girls her age are entering their freshman year of high school, complete with discussions about boys and all the latest fashions, Thessalonika has been focused on more important matters. She has been attending college since she was 11.

Brittney Exline, Youngest African American Female Accepted into an Ivy League School

Brittney graduated from Palmer High School, Colorado Springs, Colorado, in 2007 at the age of 15 with an International Baccalaureate diploma. She was then accepted to the University of Pennsylvania and became the youngest African-American female ever to be accepted to an Ivy League institution. She completed an internship at a small hedge fund on Wall Street at the age of 16, and at 17 she received the opportunity to go to Cameroon for the summer and work with One Laptop per Child.

Chapter One: The Best of Black Females

Grace Bush, Florida Teen, Graduates College before High School

Grace Bush, a 16-year-old Florida teen earned a bachelor's degree in criminal justice from Florida Atlantic University a week before getting her high school diploma from Florida Atlantic University High School. Bush is part of her school's dual enrollment program, which allows high-performing high school students to earn credit for the same courses toward their college degree. She started at age 13 at Broward College and took classes throughout the summer, so she was able to finish it before four years. "It's kind of weird that I graduated college before high school," Bush said. She plans to pursue a master's degree and hopes to attend law school. Her goal is to someday become the chief justice of the U.S. Supreme Court.

Teen Chess Champion Rochelle Ballantyne

Rochelle Ballantyne, from Brooklyn, New York, was featured in the 2012 chess documentary, *Brooklyn Castle*. The movie tells the stories of five members of the chess team at a below-the-poverty-line inner city junior high school that has won more national championships than any other in America. Rochelle no longer attends I.S. 318 Middle School (the movie finished filming in 2010), but she still continues to play and strives to reach her goal of becoming the first African-American female master.

Chapter One: The Best of Black Females

Gabrielle Turnquest, Youngest Person to Pass The Bar

At 16, **Gabrielle Turnquest,** an American teenager has become the youngest person in more than 600 years to become a qualified barrister in England and Wales. The average lawyer passes the Bar Professional Training Course at the age of 27, but Gabrielle was called to The Bar last month through the Honourable Society of Lincoln's Inn after passing her Graduate Diploma in Law at the University of Law when she was just 17. She doesn't plan on using her success to work as a barrister in the UK; instead, she plans on returning to the U.S. in fall of 2014. Gabrielle already made history at Liberty University in Virginia, where she became the youngest student to gain an undergraduate degree, in psychology, at the age of 16. Now that she's passed The Bar, Gabrielle is to attend the Fashion Institute of Design and Merchandising in a bid to break into the niche market of fashion law. Gabrielle also hopes to sit the multi-state Bar in the U.S.

Chapter Two: Trends

I have always loved numbers, math, and statistics because of their power to tell a story. In this chapter, we will take a quantitative look at the challenges facing Black girls. This data will serve as the framework through which we examine the challenges and the driving force behind the implementation of strategies that have proven effective.

NAEP Grade 8 Reading

	Below	Basic	Proficient	Advanced
Alabama	41	46	13	0
Arizona	33	43	24	1
Arkansas	47	40	12	0
California	35	47	16	2
Colorado	31	39	26	4
Connecticut	30	47	22	1
Delaware	28	48	23	1
DC	46	38	15	1
Florida	36	46	18	1
Georgia	33	49	17	1
Illinois	32	48	19	1
Indiana	31	49	18	1
Kansas	32	49	18	1
Kentucky	35	49	16	0
Louisiana	44	43	12	0
Maryland	29	47	22	2
Massachusetts	49	42	26	3
Michigan	40	46	14	1
Minnesota	38	44	17	0
Mississippi	44	46	10	0
Missouri	39	46	15	0
Nebraska	35	43	21	1
Nevada	30	46	21	4
New Jersey	26	45	28	1
New York	30	48	20	2
North Carolina	31	49	19	1
Ohio	31	50	18	1
Oklahoma	39	48	12	0
Pennsylvania	43	41	15	0
Rhode Island	33	43	22	2
South Carolina	36	49	15	0
Tennessee	47	39	14	1
Texas	34	48	18	1
Virginia	33	46	19	2
Washington	16	49	34	1
West Virginia	38	37	22	2
Wisconsin	44	43	13	0
National	35	47	17	1
White Female	12	41	41	6

NAEP Grade 8 Math

	Below	Basic	Proficient	Advanced
Alabama	60	32	7	0
Arizona	37	41	20	2
Arkansas	56	37	7	1
California	55	31	13	2
Colorado	37	49	12	2
Connecticut	53	39	7	1
Delaware	42	43	14	1
DC	54	33	11	1
Florida	53	35	11	1
Georgia	45	42	12	2
Illinois	49	41	9	0
Indiana	46	43	10	1
Kansas	45	43	11	1
Kentucky	54	35	10	2
Louisiana	50	39	10	1
Maryland	43	38	16	3
Massachusetts	34	41	22	3
Michigan	67	26	7	1
Minnesota	44	37	17	2
Mississippi	57	35	8	0
Missouri	58	34	8	0
Nebraska	58	34	8	0
Nevada	59	34	6	1
New Jersey	33	46	17	3
New York	44	42	13	2
North Carolina	41	44	13	2
Ohio	51	38	10	1
Oklahoma	50	43	7	0
Pennsylvania	53	39	8	1
Rhode Island	59	36	6	0
South Carolina	48	38	13	1
Tennessee	66	26	7	1
Texas	24	52	21	3
Virginia	40	40	18	2
Washington, D.C.	38	43	18	1
West Virginia	59	36	5	0
Wisconsin	52	35	11	2
National	48	39	12	1
White Female	17	41	33	9[1]

Chapter Two: Trends

Eighty-two percent of Black females are below proficient in reading. Eighty-seven percent are below proficient in math. This is unacceptable!

Most states define "proficient" as somewhere between 60 and 75 percent. According to a survey conducted by the National Assessment of Educational Progress (NAEP), 82 percent of Black girls are below proficient in reading. This is catastrophic. I could write an entire book just on this one fact. Where is the outrage? Why aren't White feminists advocating on behalf of Black girls? Why aren't African American men—educators, researchers, scholars, activists, media pundits, and policy makers—channeling their fury into improving the reading scores of Black girls?

One answer is that the test scores of African American males have dominated our attention. Ninety percent of Black boys nationwide in eighth grade are below proficient in reading. Let me translate. That means only 10 percent of Black boys are proficient in reading. Only 18 percent of Black girls are proficient in reading. How can we live in the richest country in the world, yet only 18 percent of Black girls in eighth grade are proficient in reading?

Furthermore, according to the NAEP, 87 percent of Black girls are either below proficient or basic in math. That means only 13 percent of Black girls nationwide in eighth grade are proficient in math. Eighty-eight percent of African American males are either below proficient or basic in math. So historically, we have put nearly all our focus on African American males while overlooking African American females. We can no longer afford to continue this neglect of Black girls. While Black males may be on life support, it's not much better for Black females, who are in critical condition.

Are these statistics acceptable to American educators? When will these statistics become unacceptable? How bad does it have to get? If you thought that all was well with Black females, you are sadly mistaken. All is not well, and there is much room for improvement in these two foundational subjects. Later, when we discuss educational challenges and solutions, we will look at what must be done to improve the reading and numeracy skills of Black girls.

Retention

Too many African American students are retained. Twenty-nine percent of African American male students are retained at least once between kindergarten and eighth grade.[2] This retention figure has received national attention. What you may not know is that 21 percent of Black females are retained.[3] While Black females are not being retained as often as Black males, 21 percent is nothing to celebrate. In fact, it's a tragedy. In comparison, 10 percent of students of other races are retained, which means the retention rate of Black females is twice as high. Where is the outrage and concern from White feminists and African American educators?

Later in the book, we will look at retention from several different prisms. For example, some retained students are assigned the same teacher, the same lesson plans, the same pedagogy, and the same expectations in the next school year. In other words, the student receives the same learning program, yet she is expected to produce a different outcome. This borders on insanity.

The so-called "social promotion" is another problematic strategy that fails to meet the academic needs of students. Many schools have decided that rather than retain students, they will promote them to the next grade so that they can continue to be grouped with their peers. What sense does this make? They haven't mastered the skills required in the current grade level! How will they keep up in the higher grade level? This is exactly the kind of school practice that plants seeds of student frustration that can lead to dropping out. Can you imagine how frustrating it is for a ninth-grade student to be in high school with fourth-grade reading and math skills? It is equally disappointing for the ninth-grade teacher.

ACT Scores

While African American males are scoring an abysmal 16.8 on the ACT, again, all is not well with African American females, who are only scoring 17.1.[4] Please remember that the highest score to be earned on the ACT is 36. The median national score is 23. This 17.1 score tells us that less than 40 percent of African American females are college ready. If we look at being college ready in all four subjects—language arts, writing, math, and science—less than 10 percent of Black girls are college ready.[5] Where is the outrage?

Chapter Two: Trends

Dropout Rate

The dropout rate for African American males hovers near 47 percent,[6] and in some cities the rate exceeds 50 percent. There has been a national outcry; the country has decided that 47 percent is unacceptable. As a result, numerous programs have been created to reduce the Black male dropout rate.

What has not received national attention is the Black female dropout rate, which is 40 percent.[7] Granted, Black females' dropout rate is 7 percent below that of African American males, but 40 percent is still too high. It is unacceptable. Where is the outrage from White feminists, the African American community, and the educational community? Where are the media stories and documentaries lamenting the Black female dropout rate? When more than one-third of your students do not graduate from high school—that is a state of emergency. Later, we will look at what can be done to help more and more Black girls successfully graduate from high school.

What kind of future will Black girls have if they drop out of high school? Earlier, I asked if your school is doing anything special for Black girls. If our schools were providing special services and paying extra attention to girls deemed at risk, then 40 percent of them would not want to leave.

School Suspensions/Expulsions

Twenty-four percent, or one of every four Black boys, are suspended from school.[8] This is so catastrophic that U.S. Attorney General Eric Holder and Secretary of Education Arne Duncan have held press conferences to address the fact that schools need to take another look at the school-to-prison pipeline and the disproportionate number of Black males that are suspended—because the two strongly correlate. Twenty-four percent is unacceptable.

When I discovered that 12 percent of Black girls are suspended and 8 percent are expelled from school and that Black girls are suspended and expelled four times more than White girls, I was furious.[9] This also is unacceptable. Are schools expecting Black girls to act like White girls? Are White girls the standard for Black females?

Suspensions and expulsions negatively impact time on task. How can we improve the reading, math, and ACT scores of Black girls who have been sent home, sometimes for days at a time? How can we reduce the dropout rate of Black females when so many of them are being sent home on suspension? What a mixed message schools are sending! Why has school culture become so penal? Has zero tolerance become the only disciplinary measure on the table?

College
The following stats are very interesting.
- There are 1.4 million Black males and 2.3 million Black females in college.[10]
- The graduation rate for African American males is only 35 percent and 46 percent for African American females.
- Black males are only 29 percent of Black college graduate students. African American females are 71 percent.
- Of all the college degrees earned by African Americans, Black women earned:
  - o   68 percent of associate degrees
  - o   66 percent of bachelor's degrees
  - o   71 percent of master's degrees
  - o   65 percent of doctorate degrees.[11]

I don't give schools any credit for the tremendous college achievements of young Black women. If anything, in spite of what schools have done to Black girls K–12, they have found the tenacity to overcome. In my forthcoming book, *Raising Black Girls,* we will look at how families, communities, and churches have strengthened the resiliency of our girls.

It is amazing to me that only 18 percent of girls are proficient in reading. Only 13 percent are proficient in math. They only scored 17.1 on the ACT, yet look at how successful they have been at the collegiate level. Yes, the graduation rate could be much better, but given all that they have had to overcome, I am pleased to see that more than 2.3 million Black females were admitted into college and nearly half persevered to earn their degree.

Criminal Justice System
One million African American males are involved in the penal system. We've all heard the statements that there are more Black males in prison than there are in college. The reality is that there are 1.4 million African American males in college to one million in prison.[12] The media need to get their numbers straight.

Chapter Two: Trends

There's no question that one million Black males in prison is too many, but the media loves to create fear, especially in the Black community. If Black males continue to hear that there are more Black males in prison than in college, there's a very good chance that's where they will end up.

All is not well for African American females; more than 100,000 are involved in the penal system. Although African Americans comprise only 14 percent of the U.S. population, Black males and females combined make up more than *50 percent* of prison and jail populations.[13] Again, we have heard so much about the plight of African American males in penal institutions, but many African American females are there as well. Furthermore, almost 40 percent are mothers. Have we considered the academic impact of parental incarceration on the children?

Where is the outrage? Where is the concern from White feminists, the African American community, and educators concerning this issue?

Following are some questions for you to explore in your notebook:

- How do Black youth with incarcerated mothers perform in the classroom?
- What is their emotional state?
- What is their behavior in the classroom, cafeteria, and playground?
- How can we help them overcome the stigma of having an incarcerated parent? How can we help them develop high self-esteem?
- How can we help stabilize their lives?
- How can we help them improve their academic performance?
- How can we support their primary guardians (often a grandmother, aunt, or foster parent)?

Sexually Transmitted Diseases

Nationwide, one of every four girls has an STD. One of every three Black males has an STD. But one of every two Black girls has an STD.[14] *One of every two Black girls.* This is a national health crisis of epic proportions. Where is the outrage? When do these figures become unacceptable?

Let's recap what we learned in this chapter:

- 82 percent of Black girls are below proficient in reading.

- 87 percent are below proficient in math.
- 21 percent of Black girls are retained.
- ACT scores average 17.1.
- Less than 40 percent of Black girls are college ready.
- Less than 10 percent are college ready in all four subjects (language arts, writing, math, and science).
- 40 percent of Black girls drop out.
- 12 percent of Black girls are suspended.
- 8 percent are expelled.
- 2.3 million Black females are in college.
- The college graduation rate for Black females is 46 percent.
- Of all African Americans who earn degrees, Black females earn 68 percent of associate degrees, 66 percent of bachelor's degrees, 71 percent of master's degrees, and 65 percent of doctorate degrees.
- There are more than 100,000 Black females in prison or jail.
- One of every two Black females has an STD.

In the next chapter, we will listen to Black females and honor their voices.

Chapter Three: Black Females Speak

Over the past year, I have traveled the country and listened to Black female students share their desires, dreams, challenges, and frustrations. I have tried to write them down exactly as they spoke, in their vernacular. Each of their thoughts could generate another book.

I encourage educators and others reading this book to reflect on each thought. Educators should discuss these ideas at staff meetings. Black girls are on point regarding their perceptions of the educational experience. Their voices are important, and they need to be heard and respected.

In your school, are Black girls listened to? Are their voices respected, honored, cherished, and valued?

Listed below are some of the thoughts of Black girls. Make sure to jot down ideas in your notebook, and share them with your colleagues.

- Why do boys get more attention?
- Why do teachers call on boys more than girls?
- Why do most teachers punish girls faster than boys?
- Why do teachers think I'm loud?
- Why do girls get suspended for talking to each other?
- Why do we fight so much?
- I don't want to go to school.
- I like Mrs. Brown. She's smart, a good teacher.

She's fair, pretty, dresses nice, and owns her own business.

• Why do teachers think I have an attitude?

• I think teachers have an attitude and some don't want to be in this school.

• I wish we had a Black female teacher in algebra and biology.

• In this school you can get suspended over your attitude.

• Why don't teachers understand me?

- Your lectures are boring.
- Why don't teachers listen to me?
- I don't want to go to college. I want to be a beautician.
- I like Mrs. Johnson because she makes it relevant.
- I wish I could go to a magnet school or a private school.
- I got suspended for rolling my eyes at a teacher.
- I want to read about Black women in the textbook.
- The bathrooms are filthy, and the food is nasty.

- I want to read Black female writers.
- Don't make me have to take off my earrings.
- Why don't teachers let me write about what I like?
- Girls need mentors, too.
- Can we have separate classes from boys?
- I like Mr. Robbins because he makes us do the work.
- Why do they call us bossy while boys are good leaders?
- Teachers should use YouTube more.

- Stop the boys from touching me.
- Why do some teachers holler at me and embarrass me in class?
- Stop girls from fighting and bullying me.
- Prepare me for college.
- Teach me how to study.
- Help me with my science project.
- Convince me that my science project will be better than the boys'.
- This school feels like a jail.

- Do some White teachers want me to talk and act like White girls?
- Raise your expectations.
- I like Mrs. Brown because I can talk to her during her lunch.
- Give me more homework.
- Do you care enough about me to visit my house?
- We need more computers in this school.
- The curriculum is boring, White, and no females.
- Help me to be a better writer.
- Dress like a professional.

- I am sick of teachers calling on light skinned girls with weave more than dark skinned girls with real hair.
- Why don't teachers like me?
- Teach me how to do a research paper.
- I don't like biology because I hate dissecting animals.
- Why don't schools promote Black colleges?
- You have to connect with me before you can correct me.
- Why do we fight over boys and they don't fight over us?

- How can I be in algebra and don't know my multiplication tables?

- I like Mrs. Jackson because she teaches us Black history in English class.

- You know the boys like our juicy fruit.

- Who gossips to you will gossip about you.

- Word is bond.

- How can I be in eighth grade and can barely read?

- I would go to college if I had the money.

- What do you think I will be doing at age 30?
- I would rather date a baller than a nerd.
- I may not go to college because I took the SAT late and just turned in my application.
- Don't ignore me because I'm quiet.
- I like sports, but I don't want to sweat out my perm.
- Why is there so much girl drama in this school?
- I like Mrs. Smith because she knows how to calm me down.

- I wish we had a Black female principal.
- Make me turn off my iPod in class.
- Don't let me sleep in class.
- Don't let me text, Facebook, Tweet, Snapchat, and Instagram in class.
- I would play sports, but I don't want some female trying to make me her woman.
- I can't go to college because my GPA is jacked.
- I hate the school uniform. Why do we have to wear pants all year?

- Teach me how to become a woman. Tell me how you became a woman.

- Is it easier being a White woman than a Black woman?

- I don't like textbooks and worksheets. I learn better if you explain it to me or let me do it.

- Why do males in sports receive more money?

- Why doesn't my school offer physics and calculus?

- I've had four principals in four years.

- I had five algebra teachers in one year and none who were certified.

- I like Mrs. Robertson because she divides class into groups: boys vs. the girls, and we always win.

- I'm tired of boys calling me a B and teachers doing nothing about it.

- This school would rather suspend you than educate you.

- I bet half the freshmen won't graduate.

- I need a math and science teacher who will work with me. No one in my family is good at math and science.
- Are boys smarter than girls in math and science?
- There is not one Black female poster on the wall in this school.
- I can read, but I have a problem with comprehension.
- I get nervous taking tests.
- How do algebra and geometry relate to my world?
- Encourage me to graduate.
- I want to be like Beyoncé.

- Do White teachers like us?
- I want to own my own business.
- Some teachers act like they are afraid of us.
- Are there any famous Black women other than Harriet Tubman and Rosa Parks?
- I like Mr. Ryan because he invites speakers to motivate us.
- Why do teachers sit females near bad boys to keep the peace? They affect my concentration.

- I have goals, but I don't know how to reach them and I don't know who to ask.

- I just need somebody to talk to.

- After I was raped, I was never the same student. He took away my purpose and joy.

- Schools want us to snitch, but teachers don't snitch on each other.

- I tried telling teachers about someone bullying me but they don't do jack!

• A White girl can do the same thing we do and she gets a warning and I get a three-day suspension. That's not right, it's not fair.

• This school is racist and afraid to admit it.

• You can't trust girls. They always turn on you.

• Most of my teachers don't care about me and won't be back next year.

• If you don't fight, you get viewed as a punk.

- You got to have some home-girls, in case you get rolled on.
- Don't talk about my mother.
- I will check a girl for disrespecting me, but I am not fighting over a boy.
- Without the crowd surrounding us the fight has no meaning and I could walk away.
- Don't make me take off my weave.

Chapter Three: Black Females Speak

Do any of these comments sound familiar to you? Black girls are trying to tell us something. Better yet, I think they have told us something. For the remainder of the book, we will attempt to address some of these comments.

I encourage you to address these comments in staff meetings and the teachers' lounge. We will reduce suspension and dropout rates and improve academic performance when we take the concerns that Black girls have shared with us seriously.

In the next chapter, we will look at the wide array of school options that are available to Black girls.

Chapter Four: School Demographics

No discussion of school demographics would be complete, without at least a mention of the families that populate the schools. Contrary to popular belief, the Black family is not monolithic, and Black students attend a wide variety of schools. In my forthcoming book, *Raising Black Girls,* I will delve more deeply into the family demographics of Black girls, including single-, two-parent, and extended family households, the educational background of parents, family income, and parental involvement in school.

Black families come in different sizes and income brackets. They live in the inner city, the suburbs, and rural communities. One girl's parents may have a combined income of more than $200,000. Both parents have graduate degrees, and they are actively involved in their daughter's education. The student's suburban school is the best in the state.

In the same state, another Black girl is in foster care, the juvenile system, or is being reared by an older sibling, aunt, or grandparent. There is little to no stability in her life. Her single parent may be incarcerated or homeless. The parent lacks a high school diploma and is not involved in the student's education. She attends the worst school in the state.

My work is geared toward both students and all those in between. Many educators try to convince me that their success, their efficacy, is dependent on the number of parents in the home, their educational background, income, and involvement in school. They say, "What can we do when the parent is single, low income, lacks a high school diploma, and is not involved in her child's education?" I believe these are factors to overcome. We should always keep our eyes focused on the prize, regardless of the family and community demographics of students. In addition, coming from a high-income, two-parent family does not automatically guarantee academic success. There are large numbers of Black girls living in affluent two-parent families attending hostile schools discouraging them from AP and honors classes. There are too many factors that can make or break a student's academic performance. However, since the risks are higher in impoverished communities, later in the book I'll present several examples of schools that continuously produce successful high-achieving students in high risk communities. I encourage you to study their approaches, and share them with your colleagues.

But, let's return to the wide array of school experiences that are available to our girls.

Student	Percentile in Reading and Math, State Exam	Type of School
Denise	35	Low-achieving, public
Cathy	80	High-achieving, magnet, public
Diane	50	Moderately achieving, charter
Linda	80	Private boarding
Natasha	90	High-achieving, single gender, public
Kenya	65	High-achieving, African-centered, charter
Barbara	60	High-achieving, STEM, charter
Donna	50	Moderate achieving, private
Keisha	82	Home schooled

Thus the different types of schools experienced by Black girls are:
- Low-achieving public schools
- Moderate-achieving public schools
- High-achieving public schools
- Low-achieving charter schools
- Moderate-achieving charter schools
- High-achieving charter schools
- Low-achieving single gender schools
- Moderate-achieving single gender schools
- High-achieving single gender schools
- Low-achieving African-centered schools
- Moderate-achieving African-centered schools
- High-achieving African-centered schools
- Low-achieving STEM schools
- Moderate-achieving STEM schools
- High-achieving STEM schools
- Low-achieving magnet schools
- Moderate-achieving magnet schools
- High-achieving magnet schools
- Low-achieving private schools
- Moderate-achieving private schools
- High-achieving private schools
- Low-achieving boarding schools
- Moderate-achieving boarding schools
- High-achieving boarding schools

Chapter Four: School Demographics

- Low-achieving home school
- Moderate-achieving home school
- High-achieving home school

Unfortunately, Denise's educational experience is the dominant type faced by Black girls. They're scoring in the 35th percentile, and they attend low-achieving public schools. Clearly, all Black girls should have equal access to a quality education, regardless of where they live and family circumstances.

Racial Makeup of Students

Schools can range from as low as one percent to as high as 100 percent African American students. While writing this book, I read about the brilliant actor and star of *Akeelah and the Bee*, Keke Palmer. Keke attended a school where less than five percent of the students were Black. She said it was difficult for her and she seldom was invited to social events. Girls teased her, but the challenges she endured ultimately made her stronger. She has excelled academically, athletically, and as an actor.

Can you imagine what it's like for the only Black girl in her kindergarten class to be teased by White girls about the texture of her hair and the insensitive White female teacher does not come to her rescue? Whether they are dark, light, or all shades in between, this happens to Black girls of *all* hues. Ironically, the discussions about "good" hair and "pretty" eyes and hue can be just as vicious in a kindergarten class that's 100 percent African American, and the teasing occurs to Black girls of *all* hues. The prejudice and ignorance can be the same in both classrooms, but the racial makeup is different.

The racial make-up of faculty and staff is critical. In schools, where Black students are the majority, staff may be less than 20 percent African American. Nationwide, African Americans are 18 percent of the students in public schools, but only six percent of teachers are African American.[15] Many Black girls can go K–12 and not experience an African American teacher, much less an African American *woman* teacher. They may never experience an algebra, geometry, trig, biology, chemistry, or physics class taught by an African American woman.

I've consulted at schools where the entire faculty was White, while the custodial and food service workers were all African American. Remember our student Denise mentioned above? She attends a low-achieving public school with a racial make-up of more than 80 percent African American students and less than 20 percent African American teachers. Could this be one of the reasons why Denise scored in the 35th percentile? At the very least, this race-gender staff dynamic can negatively impact the self-esteem of Black girls. Unfortunately, too many Black girls attend low-achieving schools and are taught by mostly White teachers, some of whom don't understand them or their culture. Later, when we discuss educational challenges and school solutions, we will look at the impact of race and gender on African American girls.

Location

How many students attend inner city schools? Suburban schools? Rural schools? About 65 percent of African American girls attend inner city schools, 25 percent suburban schools, and 10 percent rural schools.[16]

There is a big difference between attending a New York City high school with more than 3,000 students and a high school in rural Mississippi, with less than 300 students. The inner city is different from suburbs, rural communities, and small towns.

The major concern of some students is not about whether they pass algebra, geometry, or trigonometry. It's about them trying to safely pass through the five blocks of gang territory to get to school. Although not all Black girls live in the inner city, too many attend schools in communities filled with crime and drugs. I have spoken in hundreds of inner-city schools that remind me of prisons. I have seen girls go through metal detectors along with their possessions and yet they were patted down all over their bodies by male security staff. How can you master algebra after this daily humiliating experience? Schools should not allow male security guards to touch female students. Most girls in middle –class schools can resolve their conflicts socially. Unfortunately, in many lower-income schools, conflicts are resolved physically, which increases suspensions.

Take another look at the reading chart in the Trends chapter. Notice that not all states are ranked equally. Granted, I'm not pleased with any of the states, but I do want to show a contrast. In the state of Mississippi, less than 10 percent of the students were proficient in reading. In the state of Washington, 34 percent of Black girls were proficient or above in reading.

Chapter Four: School Demographics

In West Virginia, less than five percent of Black girls were proficient or above in math. But in Massachusetts, more than 22 percent were proficient in math.

Please don't misunderstand me. In my opinion, the state of Washington needs to improve. Thirty-four percent is unacceptable. Massachusetts' 22 percent in math is unacceptable. However, 34 is better than 10, and 22 is better than five. Ironically, a child in Mississippi who attends a high-achieving public, magnet, charter, boarding, single-gender, African-centered, STEM, private, or home school can outperform a student who attends a low-achieving public school in Washington or Massachusetts. Location does not necessarily ensure that students will be high achieving. Location is simply one variable, but is not the most important.

In fact, most states are guilty of unequal distribution of funding. Unfortunately, most schools are funded by property taxes. Schools in affluent suburbs may allocate $20,000 per student, while schools in the inner city or rural communities may allocate less than $9,000 per student. In affluent suburbs, every child has a computer, and every teacher has a master's degree and higher. In the inner city and rural communities, one computer lab may serve 600 students; math and science teachers are often uncertified in those disciplines. Nationwide, only 50 percent of high schools offer calculus and 63 percent offer physics. Nationwide, 25% of schools primarily in the inner city or rural communities do not offer algebra II or chemistry.[17] For some reason, our society and the U.S. Supreme Court do not have a problem with this form of affirmative action for K–12. We have abolished affirmative action at the collegiate level and naïvely believe all students have a level K–12 playing field. Our society has no intention of closing the racial academic achievement gap. For that reason, it continues to impress me that so many schools have created a positive school culture and closed the racial academic achievement gap. They have succeeded in spite of the superintendent, school board, unions, city council, mayor, and poor parent demographics.

Some states allocate less than 30 percent of the school budget and the balance comes from property taxes. On the other hand, in Vermont and Hawaii, more than 90 percent of the school budget is paid by the state.[18] So if Black girls attended schools in Vermont and Hawaii (unfortunately, there are few Black girls in those states), they would receive an education that is at least adequately funded.

However, even adequate funding doesn't mean that schools in Vermont, Hawaii, Washington, and Massachusetts are high achieving. With too few African American teachers who care about them, Black girls might still be underperforming. A Black female could attend a school in the above four states and be given lower expectations and tracked to lower classes. This same student could attend the best schools in Mississippi or West Virginia where they are nurtured, respected and given high expectations.

School Culture

I believe the most important variable for Black girls is the culture of the school. In my book *Changing School Culture for Black Males,* I emphasize the importance of culture in schools. Note, I didn't say the racial make-up of the staff, the educational background or income level of parents, the location of the school, or funding. I believe the most important factor affecting the education of Black girls is school culture. School culture conveys a certain feeling that can be detected the moment you walk through the doors. It communicates a message and quality of life and learning, and it powerfully influences all who teach and learn there. School culture can be either negative or positive.

Much more will be said about culture in the chapter on school solutions, but in the meantime, write your answers to the following questions in your notebook. Improving your school culture will be an excellent topic for the teachers' lounge and staff meetings. I would love to work with your staff on this crucial issue.

- Is the culture in your school negative or positive?
- Are teachers pessimistic or optimistic?
- Are parents always welcome at your school and in your classroom?
- Do teachers believe external factors in the home and community have more power over girls than internal factors in the school?
- Do teachers put forth their best effort in the classroom?
- How do teachers talk about students and their families in the teachers' lounge?
- Do you have low or high expectations of your students?
- Is your principal an instructional leader or an office-bound CEO?
- Are your students allowed to waste time sleeping, listening to music, braiding hair, etc.?
- Is your curriculum Eurocentric and patriarchal?

Chapter Four: School Demographics

- Would you send your child to your school?
- Which teachers would you prohibit teaching your child?

Time on Task

In some schools, students are academically engaged for six or seven hours per day. In other schools, students spend less than four hours academically engaged. Some schools are open 180 days during the school year. Other schools are open for business 200 days throughout the year.

Time spent academically engaged or disengaged has a way of adding up. How do students at your school spend their time? Are they learning all day long? Are they excited and engaged about their class work? During study periods are they actually studying?

Unfortunately, too many Black girls attend low-achieving schools where they are allowed to listen to music in class. They're texting, emailing, Tweeting, posting to Facebook, Instagram, and Snapchat, or even sleeping. Study periods are for braiding hair and talking about everything but class work. Teachers spend more time disciplining students than educating them. I've found that students in low-achieving schools are academically disengaged as much as *one-third* of the class period. Those hours are precious and can never be retrieved. Lost hours result in below proficient reading and math scores. I could write an entire book just on the power of time on task.

Imagine two teachers at a school in Anytown, USA. Same community, same school, same subject, same time allotment for the class period. Teacher 1 is on fire, loves and knows her subject thoroughly, and is so connected with her students; they are completely engaged for the entire 50-minute period. Teacher 2 spends the first five minutes taking attendance. She spends the next few minutes trying to calm her students down, practically begging them to be quiet, stop texting, etc. She hands out worksheets and tells them to answer the questions. No discussion, no interesting stories about the subject matter, nothing. The bell rings, and the thoroughly disengaged students are running for the door. The first teacher produces a 1.5 percent annual increase in test scores. The latter teacher produces a .5 percent annual increase.[19] The students are still Black from single parent low-income homes without degrees and very little involvement, but with the first group, if they have teachers like Teacher 1 from first through eighth grades, they will have 12th-grade test scores while the latter group will have fourth-grade scores.

Consider summer vacation. Many schools still design the school calendar on the old agrarian model and are closed during the three months of summer. What happens to students during those three months? Well, some will continue learning by going to the library, museums, and the zoo. They'll travel the world, read books, and attend academic, athletic, music instruction, and other skills-building camps. Other students won't be as fortunate. They will have too much unsupervised time on their hands with nothing to do but play and "hang out."

Three months (of summer) times 12 years (grades 1–12) equals 36 months or three years. That's precious time! Those three years can mean the difference between graduating and not graduating from high school. Three years of supervised academic engagement can serve as a safety net for girls at risk of dropping out. Three years of attending supervised camps, summer school, etc., could save many Black female students from not only scoring below proficient scores in reading and math, but out-of-wedlock pregnancies and STDs.

There has been much debate over the years about the so-called "three-year gap" between Black and White students. Three years of lost time during the summer months across elementary, middle, and high school help explain this gap. Too many Black girls are academically disengaged during the summer. If we're going to raise the bar and improve academic achievement for Black girls, we not only have to keep them on task during the school day and throughout the school year, we must keep them academically engaged during the summer months. I recommend mandatory summer school for all students scoring below proficient.

We have large numbers of Black females attending excellent schools with nurturing teachers who have high expectations and an optimistic school culture. The problem is we have far too many Black females attending schools where teachers are hostile and have low expectations, are uncertified and extremely transient, and the school culture has convinced them the problems are external and beyond their control.

In the next chapter, we will look at what I think is one of the most important chapters in this book: STEM. We must introduce STEM to Black girls. Begin today, by letting your Black female students know that they can become a doctor, dentist, computer programmer, systems analyst, accountant, engineer, and so much more.

Chapter Five: STEM

In general, women are underrepresented in science, technology, engineering, and mathematics (STEM) career fields. According to the American Community Survey women are 48 percent of the U.S. workforce, but just 24 percent of workers in STEM fields. Women with STEM jobs earned 33 percent more than women in non-STEM jobs. As a result, the gender wage gap is smaller in STEM jobs than in non-STEM jobs.

If women in general are underrepresented in STEM, African American women are practically nonexistent, especially in engineering. According to the National Science Foundation:

- Of 13,693 bachelor's degrees in engineering awarded to women, only 805 went to Black women. In comparison, 60,706 men received degrees.
- Of the 8,402 master's degrees in engineering awarded to women, Black women received 334. In comparison, 29,212 men were awarded degrees.
- There were a total of 1.6 million engineering jobs. Of the 200,000 engineering jobs held by women, Black women held 10,000 jobs.[20]

In my opinion, this is the most important chapter in the book. There's no other area where Black females have been shortchanged more than in the disciplines of math and science. Only two percent of America's doctors (20,000) and engineers (10,000) are African American women.[21] Of all the statistics that have been provided thus far in the book, the STEM statistics are the most abysmal. We must increase the number of African American females who will pursue and achieve careers in math and science.

Susan McKinney-Steward,
First African American Female MD in NY

Susan McKinney-Steward graduated from the New York Medical College for Women in 1870, a homeopathic medical school. The school was founded in 1863 by Dr. Clemence Sophia Lozier, a wealthy abolitionist who became a close friend and mentor to Susan. By studying long hours Susan earned the honor of being class valedictorian. She worked undeterred by the taunting of male medical students during clinic hours at Bellevue Hospital.

Chapter Five: STEM

Rebecca Lee Crumpler,
First African American Female to Earn an MD

In 1864, **Rebecca Crumpler** became the first African American woman in the United States to earn a medical degree, and the only African American woman to graduate from the New England Female Medical College, which merged with Boston University School of Medicine in 1873.

Mary Eliza Mahoney,
First African American Graduate Nurse

In 1878 **Mary Mahoney** became a student, at 33 years of age, in a nursing program established by Dr. Marie Zakrzewska. Sixteen months later, she was one of four students out of 42 who completed the rigorous course. She worked mainly as a private duty nurse for the next 30 years.

Chapter Five: STEM

Madame C. J. Walker,
Inventor Straightening Comb and Cosmetics

Born **Sarah Breedlove Walker,** Sarah began to lose her hair from a scalp ailment during the 1890s. Embarrassed by this condition, she experimented with a variety of homemade remedies and products. This led to the development of the first hair straightening comb and Madame Walker's Wonderful Hair Grower, a scalp conditioning and healing formula. She also was one of the first women, White or Black, to become a millionaire on her own.

May Edward Chinn,
First African American Female Intern at Harlem Hospital,
Cancer Researcher

The daughter of a runaway slave, **May Chinn** did not plan to become a doctor. She originally wanted to be a musician, but she changed to science after earning a medical degree. In 1926 she became the first African American woman to graduate from Bellevue Medical College and then she became the first African American female intern at Harlem Hospital in New York City. She was also known for her research on cancer. She founded an organization in 1975 which promotes African American women's interest in attending medical school.

Chapter Five: STEM

Ruth Ella Moore,
First African American Female PhD in Bacteriology

Ruth Ella Moore earned her doctorate in the field of bacteriology, becoming the first African American woman in the United States to earn a PhD in the natural sciences. Ruth attended Ohio State University and earned a BS in 1926 and an MS in 1927.

Roger Arliner Young,
First African American Female Zoologist and Marine Biologist

Roger Arliner Young was the first African American woman to receive a PhD in zoology, which she did while juggling research, teaching and caring for her invalid mother. In 1916, she entered Howard University and took her first science course in 1921. Ernest Everett Just, a prominent black biologist and head of the zoology department at Howard University, recognized her promise and became her mentor. Although she had poor grades, Roger graduated with a BS in 1923 and a PhD in 1927.

Chapter Five: STEM

Helen Octavia Dickens,
First African American Female in the American
College of Surgeons

At 12 years old, encouraged by her family, her dentist and a secretary at the local YWCA, **Helen Octavia Dickens** decided to pursue a medical career. In 1934 she was the only African American woman in her graduating class at the University of Illinois School of Medicine. In 1943, she took a year's concentration in obstetrics and gynecology at Penn Graduate School of Medicine. She was the first African American female in the American College of Surgeons.

Dorothy Lavinia Brown,
First African American Female Surgeon in the South

Dorothy Lavinia Brown was the first African American female surgeon in the South. At only five months old, her unmarried mother placed her in the Troy Orphanage. By 1948, Dorothy had attended Meharry Medical College in Nashville, TN, graduating in the top third of her class.

Chapter Five: STEM

Jewel Plummer Cobb,
PhD in Cell Physiology, Melanin Research
and Cancer Treatment

A cell biologist and cell physiologist, known for her work with skin pigment, or melanin, **Jewel Plummer Cobb** has encouraged women and ethnic minorities to enter the sciences throughout her career. In 1950 she earned a PhD in cell physiology from New York University. Her research, known for how drugs affect cancer cells, has contributed greatly to the field of chemotherapy.

Jocelyn Elders,
U.S. Surgeon General

Born Minnie Jones, **Jocelyn Elders** and her siblings spent their childhood laboring in the cotton fields. Jocelyn earned a scholarship to the all-Black, liberal arts Philander Smith College. Her father did not see the value of an education and did not want her to go. Upon graduation she enlisted in the U.S. Army Women's Medical Specialist Corps in 1956. She attended the Arkansas Medical School on the G.I. Bill and became US Surgeon General in 1986.

Chapter Five: STEM

Jane Cooke Wright,
First African American Female Associate Dean of a
Medical School and President, the NY Cancer Society

Jane Cooke Wright implemented a new comprehensive program to study stroke, heart disease, and cancer, and she created another program to instruct doctors in chemotherapy.

Alexa Canady,
First African American Female in Neurosurgery

Alexa Canady became the first African American woman to enter the field of neurosurgery in 1976 as a physician in training. Since then, Canady has become one of the top specialists in the United States. Patients of all ages with particularly baffling neurological disorders or deeply entrenched brain tumors go to her for consultation.

Chapter Five: STEM

Mae Carol Jemison,
First African American Admitted to the Astronaut
Training Program

After two years as a Peace Corps Medical Officer, **Mae Carol Jemison** decided in 1985 to follow a dream that she had nurtured for a long time. She applied for admission to NASA's astronaut training program. That year's selection was cancelled due to the Challenger disaster; but when she reapplied a year later, Jemison was one of the 15 chosen and the first African American ever selected into the training. She has printed wiring board materials, and has worked in computer programming, nuclear magnetic resonance spectroscopy, computer magnetic disc production, and reproductive biology.

Dale Emeagwali,
NTA's Scientist of the Year in Microbiology, Molecular Biology and Biochemistry

Dale Emeagwali excels in the fields of microbiology, molecular biology, fermentation, enzymology, virology, cell biology, and biochemistry. She earned a Scientist of the Year award for her work in cancer research. As a minority in a primarily White field she has been commended for her contributions to and accomplishments in medical science. She also works to expose minority youth to the sciences.

Chapter Five: STEM

Theoretical Physicist Dr. Shirley Ann Jackson

An assistant principal at her segregated high school pointed **Dr. Shirley Ann Jackson** toward Massachusetts Institute of Technology. But as the first Black woman to attend the prestigious technical college in 1964, Jackson was the target of discrimination. Some students refused to sit near her, and one faculty member suggested she "learn a trade." Instead of feeling sorry for herself, Jackson responded by volunteering in the children's ward of a local hospital to keep things in perspective. Undaunted, she focused on physics. She became the first Black woman to obtain a PhD from MIT and the first in the nation to earn a doctorate in physics. Dr. Shirley Ann Jackson added yet another first to her résumé when she became the first African American and the first woman to chair the United States Nuclear Regulatory Commission in 1995. Dr. Jackson continues to make history today as the first African American woman to lead a national research university, Rensselaer Polytechnic Institute in Troy, New York.

President and CEO of Morehouse School of Medicine, Dr. Valerie Montgomery Rice

Set to become the incoming president and CEO of Morehouse School of Medicine on July 1, 2014, **Dr. Valerie Montgomery Rice** will be the first African American woman at the top position of a freestanding medical school. She will also maintain her role as the medical school's dean. A native of Georgia, she received her bachelor's degree in chemistry from Georgia Institute of Technology and her medical degree from Harvard Medical College. Her specialties in infertility research, her founding of the Center for Women's Health Research at Meharry Medical College, and her leadership on issues about diseases and their impact on women of color have made her a renowned woman in her field.

Chapter Five: STEM

One of every two Black girls has an STD, but only two percent of America's doctors are African American women. Wouldn't it be great if one of every two African American females pursued and achieved a career in STEM?

There are five major variables that impact the desire of Black girls to pursue STEM degrees and careers:
- Interest
- Confidence
- Expectations
- Learning Styles
- Relevance

To increase the number of African American women in STEM fields, we must address these variables as early as the primary grades.

Making STEM Interesting

The following chart lists traditional and nontraditional jobs for women, along with potential earnings:

Career	Income (per year)
Child care worker	$18,000
Secretary	$24,000
Engineer	$155,000
Doctor	$250,000

This chart should be posted on the walls of every school that has a Black female student population. Our girls need to see the variance in income between traditional jobs and STEM careers. Dr. Mae Jemison, the brilliant scientist, NASA astronaut, and first African American woman to travel in space, said, "If we can send people to the moon, why can't we teach students science?"[22] How is it we can send ships to the planets in our solar system, but we don't know how to teach Black girls to love and master science? For more background on this important subject, read *Science for Girls* by Susan Goetz and *Sisters in Science* by Diann Jordan, both excellent books.

Unfortunately, science is taking a back seat in many schools to reading and math. Schools have become test taking factories. Education is political and many educators are politicians. They determine how many hours students will receive in each subject. Unfortunately, large numbers of Black children are being denied science and the arts. The entire school year for Black and low-income students has been reduced to evaluating how well students are doing exclusively in reading and math. Science, a very important subject for all students, especially Black girls, is only receiving an hour or two per week. If we as a nation are serious about being competitive globally, we must increase the number of hours dedicated to the teaching of science. In addition to classroom lectures and lab work, science will come alive for Black girls when they go on field trips, participate in science fairs, and join science clubs. Science teachers should be encouraged to develop science-based, cross-learning projects in English, history, and math. Have Black women scientists come and speak to your girls about their work on a monthly or quarterly basis.

In inner city, low-achieving public schools, more than 30 percent of the teachers *attempting* to teach math and science are not certified in those fields.[23] Many of those schools, which have high populations of African American students, require only one year of math (algebra) and one year of science (biology). How can our students hope to compete with their wealthy suburban counterparts who are taking four years of math, four years of science, and if they qualify, AP math and science courses? Moreover, while our girls are hanging out during the three hot months of summer, suburban students are attending computer camps, coding camps, math camps, science camps, robotics camps, and even NASA camp.

How can African American girls hope to become scientists, doctors, and engineers if they are only required to take one year of math and one year of science with uncertified teachers? Black females who manage to get accepted into college and who might consider a STEM degree often find that they are so behind, they must take remedial math courses just to catch up to the basic course work. This can be extremely frustrating and often causes young Black women to give up and change majors. How many Black female doctors and engineers have we lost due to the above scenario?

Another issue for Black females is image. Take a moment and visualize the average looking science teacher, whether in elementary school or high school. More than 90 percent of female students report that the average looking science teacher is White, male, and nerdy looking.[24]

It is unfortunate that Black girls and the larger society have an image of science teachers as White, male, and nerdy. Can you imagine if we had biology, chemistry, and physics teachers who looked like Lupita Nyong'o, Beyoncé, Alicia Keys, Mary J. Blige, and Halle Berry? I submit the following mandates to increase STEM degrees and careers among African American females. We must:

- Increase the number of African American females who will teach math and science.
- Make math and science attractive, cool, exciting, and popular.
- Be more creative in lesson plans and curriculum development.
- Teach math and science to a variety of learning styles, not just written and oral. Include visual, tactile and kinesthetic approaches as well.
- Work with teachers in language arts, history, and math to develop exciting, engaging, and fun science-based, cross-learning projects.
- Upgrade the image of the scientist and mathematician. Being a scientist does not mean being White, male, and a nerd. Scientists, engineers, and physicians can be attractive, cool, exciting, and popular. They can be women. They can be attractive, interesting Black women!

It is unfortunate that we can find money to send millions of people to jail, but we can't find an additional $1,000 to $5,000 stipend to encourage more African American females to teach math and science.

The NBA and NFL know they are only as strong as their weakest teams. Therefore, come draft time, they allow the weakest teams to pick their players first while the strongest teams pick last. In the educational field, we need to have our best math and science teachers assigned to the students who need them the most. It makes no sense to assign uncertified, unqualified teachers to our lowest performing students if we want to close the racial and gender achievement gap. Girls consistently complained to me that they were assigned, say, four uncertified teachers in math or science throughout the year. So not only weren't the teachers qualified, these classes had revolving doors. And of course, while the search was on for a new teacher, unqualified, uncertified, disengaged substitute teachers were babysitting these classes. Educators love telling me about high student mobility, but what about staff instability? I have never heard of such mismanagement of staff resources occurring in boarding schools, magnet schools, STEM charter schools, high-achieving public schools, private schools, or home schools.

The problems that girls, specifically Black girls, are experiencing in STEM begin early. There is no focus on STEM in preschool and the primary grades in low-achieving schools. Have you visited a toy store lately? Walk down the aisles and see if the items are co-ed. The toys for boys are blue, and the toys for girls are pink. The toys for girls are soft, and the toys for boys are hard. Toys for boys require them to take things apart and put them back together. Sounds to me like boys are being prepared for careers in engineering. Some students are given an airplane and all that is required is to install the batteries. Other schools and parents give their students and children an airplane kit filled with parts that require assembling.

Slowly but surely, however, some toy makers are catching on to the idea that girls are a brand new market regarding STEM. The following toy sites have been created just for girls:

- **GoldieBlox** (www.goldieblox.com) – Offers toys that are attractive to girls and encourages them to pursue careers in engineering and construction.
- **Roominate** (www.roominatetoy.com) – Uses dollhouses to encourage girls to pursue careers in math and science.
- **Sabotage at the Space Station** (http://smart adventuresgames.com) – S.M.A.R.T. Adventures™ math games use fun concepts to help girls attain STEM literacy and confidence at every stage in their educational career.
- **SciGirls** (http://scigirlsconnect.org) – Excellent science resource for girls.

I am so pleased at the wealth of materials that are available for those of us who are serious about encouraging girls, specifically Black girls, to pursue degrees and careers in STEM. The problem is not a lack of programs and materials. The brilliant writer and professor Dr. Ruth Brown said, "Black girls don't need programs, they need power."[25] From an educational standpoint the question becomes: Do we have the will, commitment, and fortitude to help Black girls pursue STEM?

Sexism begins early. In any preschool, kindergarten, or primary classroom, you'll see girls talking to each other, relating to each other, passing food to each other, and playing house with each other. Boys are very aggressively taking things apart and putting them back together. This is one of the major reasons why boys and girls are performing differently in math and science; boys' spatial intelligence is being developed at an early age, while girls are being developed in other areas. This early education arises from how we socialize boys and girls. We could clearly improve the spatial intelligence of girls if we encouraged them to become involved in building, deconstructing, and reassembling toys.

But spatial intelligence isn't enough. In fact, America would have us believe that girls lack math and science intelligence and their academic performance in these subjects is not competitive with boys. Not true. The reality is that up until eighth grade, girls and boys are virtually equal in their math and science test scores. So why don't girls pursue STEM degrees and careers as they get older? I believe that interest (or the lack thereof), developed from a young age, has a lot to do with it. I encourage parents and preschool and primary educators to give girls Legos®, puzzles, maps, and Rubik Cubes. Teach them how to play checkers and chess, nonviolent video games, and cards. From a vocabulary perspective, teach them words that reinforce spatial intelligence, including big, little, tall, short, empty, tiny, full, circle, square, round, rectangle, triangle, octagon, pentagon, and oval. Not only will these toys and games enhance girls' spatial intelligence, equally important, they will plant seeds of *interest*.

Two critical gate keeping subjects to math and science are algebra and biology, respectively. If I were a high school principal and only had one Black female teacher, I would have her teach either algebra or biology. Ideally, if I had two, one would teach algebra and one would teach biology. There is a good chance that if girls do not enjoy algebra, they probably will not want to pursue geometry, trigonometry, algebra II, and calculus. If they did not enjoy biology, they will not want to pursue chemistry and physics.

Let me give you an example of what many of our girls are experiencing. Sarah Wingo, a 13-year-old Black female student at North Naples Middle School in Naples, Florida, was taking a class in biology.

She's a vegetarian and a member of People for the Ethical Treatment of Animals. Sarah was not interested in dissecting frogs and explained her reasons to her female teacher. Now notice Sarah had a *female* teacher. Sarah Wingo's teacher snuck up behind her with a bag of freeze-dried frogs, dropped them on her binder, and walked away, laughing. Sarah Wingo could have been the next Dr. Mae Jemison, but with an experience like that, she probably will not want to take chemistry or physics.

Kiera Wilmot is a brilliant teenager, who desires to be an engineer. She was an honor roll student at Bartow High School in Florida. Kiera being a curious scientist, mixed tinfoil and toilet bowl cleaner in a bottle and brought it to school. The top of the bottle shot off and she was suspended, expelled, accused of being a terrorist, sent to an alternative school, arrested, and given a felony, yet she was never convicted.

Chapter Five: STEM

    In the Herstory chapter, I'll offer other examples of how insensitive teachers spoiled the educational experiences of African American female students. Black girls' test scores are competitive with boys in math and science. The million dollar question becomes: Can schools make the two gate keeping subjects, algebra and biology, engaging, attractive, and interesting enough to make girls pursue advanced subjects?

    Unfortunately, only 34 percent of high school chemistry students and 22 percent of physics students are female. Quite naturally, boys are going to outperform girls from this point on in math and science if the ratio is 34:66 in chemistry and 22:78 in physics. We cannot allow chemistry, physics, geometry, trigonometry, algebra II, and calculus to be optional. The College Board reports only 3 percent of the students who took the AP exam in computer science were African American.[26] The standard across the board in high school should be four years of math and four years of science. We cannot allow girls to drop advanced math and science classes when their grades dip and they're worried about a negative impact on their GPA. We must provide mentors and tutors who will help them across the finish line and who will not give up on them.

The last thing we should do is force girls to take classes they do not enjoy. However, the burden to make math and science more interesting is on schools and educators. I encourage you to brainstorm ideas with your colleagues on ways to make science and math classes more stimulating and relevant to female interests. What African American girl could resist the opportunity to investigate the ingredients that make up her favorite hair care and skin care products? A great experiment would be for girls to create their own products in the lab. That's chemistry!

Confidence

I encourage you to read the excellent article, "Is Math a Gift? Beliefs That Put Females at Risk," by Dr. Carol Dweck. In her article, she asks,

> Why aren't more of our brightest females pursuing careers in math and science?... In our research, we were looking at how students cope with confusion when they're learning brand new material. Confusion is a common occurrence in math and science, where, unlike most verbal areas, new material often involves completely new skills, concepts, or conceptual systems. So we created a new task for students to learn, and for half of the students we placed some confusing material near the beginning.
>
> What we found was that bright girls didn't cope as well with this confusion. In fact, the higher the girl's IQ, the worse she did. Many high IQ girls were unable to learn the material after experiencing confusion. This didn't happen to boys. For them, the higher their IQ, the better they learned. The confusion only energized them.
>
> We found that students who viewed their intellectual ability as something they could develop maintained their interest in learning and earned significantly higher grades than their peers who viewed intelligence as a gift—even though the two groups entered junior high with the same past grades and achievement test scores. What's more, the difference in grades increased continuously over the next two years.

Chapter Five: STEM

When we look within these findings at the gender story, we see that by the end of eighth grade, there is a considerable gap between females and males in their math grades—but only for those students who believed that intellectual skills are a gift. When we look at students who believed that intellectual ability could be expanded, the gap is almost gone. Actually, these males are doing a little better than their fixed ability counterparts, but the females are doing a great deal better than their counterparts (even though, again, they entered with equal math achievement). This suggests that girls who believe that intellectual abilities are just gifts do not fare well in math, but that those who think they are qualities that can be developed often do just fine.

Well, we began to think, females who believe in gifts might not only be more susceptible to setbacks, they should also be more susceptible to stereotypes. After all, stereotypes are stories about gifts—about who has them and who doesn't. So if you believe in a math gift and your environment tells you that your group doesn't have it, then that can be disheartening. But if, instead, you believe that math ability can be cultivated through your efforts, then the stereotype is less credible. It also seems more like something that can be overcome: "Maybe my group hasn't had the background, experience, and encouragement in the past, but with the right effort, strategies, and teaching, we should be able to make headway."[27]

Before I comment on this significant article, allow me to juxtapose Dr. Dweck's article with Dr. Jeffrey Howard's theory on the psychology of performance.[28] Ability, effort, luck, and tasks are the keys to Dr. Howard's model.

When you have strong self-esteem and you do well on a test, you attribute your success to either your ability or your efforts. If you have strong self-esteem and you do poorly on the test, you would never question your ability. You would realize that you need to study more. That's how winners think. Their success is attributed to their ability and efforts, and their failure reflects a lack of effort. Therefore, they realize that to succeed they need to study more.

If you have low self-esteem and do well on a test, you attribute that to either luck or the nature of the task. If you do poorly on the test, you would question your ability, and you would drop the class.

Let's now review and compare Dweck and Howard's findings. This is crucial to understanding not only the African American psyche, but the African American female psyche. In Dweck's article, both boys and girls had similar test scores and grades. IQs were relatively the same. So ability and test scores were not the issue. The issue is confidence. When boys were exposed to more challenging, confusing information, they studied harder. They didn't even consider the possibility of giving up.

Unfortunately, the girls who thought their ability to do math and science was a gift, dropped the class after becoming disillusioned with the difficult material. How many brilliant African American females have we lost to low self-confidence? Instead of buckling down and studying harder, they gave up when they believed their gift wasn't good enough.

We must help girls, especially Black girls, build their confidence. We must teach them the psychology of performance. We must teach them that success occurs with both ability and effort. Girls need to understand that when they are presented with challenging and confusing material, when they have a teacher who is difficult to understand or hard to work with, they should not drop the class. They must try a little harder. Get a tutor if necessary.

Too many African Americans believe they are better in sports than science, better with popular music than math. When you think this way, you undermine your ability to succeed. If your math teacher has low expectations of you, if you are the only African American in the class, you may begin to question your ability. Your self-doubt may increase if you're the only African American student in an AP, gifted, or honors class. Your ability may have gotten you this far, but now you're going to have to put in extra time and work. This explains why most African Americans have declining test scores after fourth grade. Their natural gift was adequate in the primary grades, but it will now require additional work in the latter grades. Black girls should know that just because STEM subjects can be confusing and challenging, that doesn't mean they don't have what it takes to master algebra, geometry, trig, calculus, biology, chemistry, and physics. They can master those subjects if they simply study longer and harder. We must teach African American girls that their innate math and science ability can be improved and expanded upon. This is critical if we are to increase the number of Black girls in STEM.

Most important, educators should study the psychology of performance for themselves and their own efficacy. If you have Black girls in your class who are difficult to work with or are having a hard time mastering the subject matter, that doesn't mean you give up on them. Don't call your efficacy into question. Your ability to teach took you this far. Now you need to roll up your sleeves and work a little harder. Spend more time with the student. Maybe you need to step out of your comfort zone and learn how to teach to a different learning style than you're used to practicing. Maybe you need to make your lesson plans more interesting and relevant to Black girls. Maybe you need to learn about the culture of your students. Remember, master teachers believe if the student has not learned the teacher has not taught. Maybe you need to reach out to parents and the community for support and advice. Whatever it takes—our girls are worth it.

Expectations

I encourage you to read the research from Teacher Expectations & Student Achievement (TESA).[29] Now take out your notebook, and answer the following questions:

- Do you believe all children *can* learn?
- Do you believe all children *will* learn?
- Do you believe Black students *can* learn math and science as well as White and Asian students?
- Do you believe Black female students *will* learn math and science as well as White and Asian male students?

If you don't believe that Black girls will learn math and science, then this is purely a theoretical exercise. As a classroom teacher, you have to believe that Black girls will learn math and science as well as White and Asian male students. Until you believe that, you should take a temporary leave of absence from your classroom because it's obvious the problem is not with Black girls, but with your expectations.

When I ask teachers if they believe that all children can learn, they say yes. Then I ask if all children *will* learn this year in their classrooms. Let's just say the answers are a bit more hesitant.

There's a tremendous difference between *can* and *will*. Furthermore, if you quantify the goal, that makes teachers accountable. For example, let's say your goal is all students will score in the 80th or 90th percentile in math and science this year. Because the goal is measurable, you can determine if students *did* learn. If the goal was met, your work in the classroom was a success. If it wasn't, you'll have to make some adjustments.

Can learn refers to the innate ability of your students. *Will learn*, however, requires your involvement in the learning process.

The TESA program offers more effective measurements than simply asking teachers if they believe all children can learn. One way to measure expectations is through the use of response opportunities. Ask yourself the following:

- Do you allow boys to dominate the discussion in your math and science classes?
- Do you call on boys more?
- Do you respond more to their hands being waved?
- Do you allow them to shout out the answers?
- Do your quiet, polite, respectful girls have fewer chances to respond?

You can't say you have the same expectations for your students when there is a wide disparity of response opportunities in your class. One solution is to put each of your students' names on index cards. Ask your question, but don't respond to boys who are hollering, standing up, and waving their hands. Instead, pick a card and call out the student's name. That way there will be an equitable distribution of response opportunities.

Language and words are powerful. I'm very concerned about the language that's used in math and science classes, especially in front of females. Do you use co-ed language, or do you refer to all students as *guys*? When you refer to a scientist, do you use co-ed language, or do you say *he*?

Images are powerful. Do you have posters of both male and female scientists, African American and others, on the walls of your classroom, or are the pictures primarily of White males? Do your textbooks depict only male scientists peering through microscopes with female assistants standing behind them?

Chapter Five: STEM

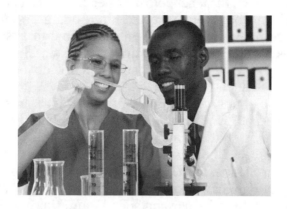

I have observed female teachers directing their male students to do the actual research while female students serve as recorders. This classroom behavior is sexist, and it starts early. Remember, secretaries are making $24,000 a year while engineers are making $155,000 and doctors are making $250,000 per year. Our language and images need to be more inclusive of female students.

When it's time to set up or put away the lab equipment, is that job equally shared between both genders, or do you have the males set up and put away the equipment, while the girls are doing secretarial work? I strongly suggest that girls set up and put away the computers, software, PowerPoint presentations, the microscope, the telescope—whatever equipment and technologies are being used. Girls need to be involved in every stage of the lesson.

We can't say we have the same expectations for girls and boys while allowing these sexist behaviors to continue. I've observed too many science labs where, instead of performing experiments, girls are in the rear of the classroom, talking to friends about things that have nothing to do with the lesson. Teachers are not helping girls when they allow them to disengage from lab work. In fact, the message they're communicating to girls is, "We know you're *not* going to become a doctor or engineer, so it doesn't matter if you do the work or not." This is unacceptable.

TESA identifies *feedback* as another way to operationalize high teacher expectations in the classroom. Research shows when a Black female student offers an incorrect answer, she is given little time to ponder. She receives few clues, reinforcement, probing,

75

or discussion from the teacher to help her arrive at a better answer. But when White boys, our expected future engineers and doctors, answer incorrectly, they are given more time to answer. More probing takes place. Deeper questions are asked. Clearly the goal is to help boys arrive at a correct answer. Girls do not receive the same quality of attention.

This call to go deeper not only helps girls arrive at better answers, the back and forth Q&A teaches them how to think critically about challenging subjects. In addition, classroom feedback reinforces the psychology of performance on the spot. In the hands of a talented master teacher, feedback says to the student, "Your ability may have gotten you this far, but you're going to have to work a little harder and spend more time on this task to truly understand the subject matter. This is how you do it. Don't give up."

If we're expecting Black girls to become more engaged with STEM subjects, we need to give them more feedback. We need to allow them more time to reconsider their answers. Boys should not be allowed to interrupt and burst out answers, and they certainly should not be allowed to make sexist, derogatory comments about girls. Allowing males to make sexist comments is a reflection of you as a teacher (and often a woman).

You can tell an awful lot about a class, especially math and science classes, from the interaction between teachers and female students. When a female student has answered incorrectly...

- How much time is she given to rethink her answer?
- Is she treated with respect for her intelligence, or is she made to feel stupid (in front of her peers, especially boys)?
- Do you probe by asking more questions? How deep are the questions?
- Do your probing questions facilitate the development of critical thinking skills?
- Do your words, tone of voice, and body language convey your belief that she *will* learn, that you *will* help her, you won't give up on her, and you *will* support her?
- Do you encourage her to never give up?
- Do you reflect on your own ability to teach to her particular learning style?

Chapter Five: STEM

Literally, we can make or break a student in the area of feedback.

There's a tremendous difference between how math and science are taught in Japan and Singapore and the United States. In the U.S., we cover a wide array of topics in math and science, which often means that students are memorizing, but not analyzing, skimming the surface, but not diving deeply into the subject matter. In Japan and Singapore, fewer concepts are covered in math and science, but the lessons take students into a deeper level of learning. If we want to improve the performance of girls in STEM, we need to study how Japan and Singapore are teaching math and science. We need to cover fewer concepts, but discuss them more deeply. Most girls are not comfortable memorizing facts, figures, and formulas without understanding their context, meaning, and relevance.

Learning Styles

There are at least five ways to learn: written, oral, visual, tactile, and kinesthetic. In the chapter on school solutions, we will look at learning styles in more detail, but suffice to say here that not all of your students, specifically Black girls, are going to respond favorably to your textbooks, worksheets, and lectures. Black girls learn in different ways. Ideally, if you are a master teacher in math or science, you will know how to meet the needs of all girls, including your oral, visual, tactile, and kinesthetic learners.

Female students usually have strong verbal skills. If they are paired with another verbal learner, they may talk the entire lesson. Ideally, they should be paired with a tactile or kinesthetic learner.

Female students often possess strong people skills, which enable them to work well with others. This is why girls perform better in cooperative learning environments, specifically single gender. While boys are busy competing against each other to lead their groups, find correct answers, and develop projects, girls are working together to achieve the same goals. There is no right or wrong, just totally different ways of relating, communicating, and learning. Since generally speaking, cooperation is a female strength, build on that. You'll find that especially in math and science classes, there is safety for girls in single gender cooperative learning. They don't have to risk looking foolish in front of boys, and under a teacher's nurturing guidance, girls will often lay aside their differences to help one another. I believe the academic performance of your female students will significantly improve in this classroom structure. I strongly encourage you to implement single gender cooperative learning groups in your classroom. This change needs to be at the top of the list.

These findings are highly significant. Cooperative learning is effective and congruent with the values, spirit, and nature of African American children, yet we continue to subject Black boys to a classroom based on the individualism and competitiveness of White culture. We no longer need to try to make African American males European and achieve academic excellence through individual effort. African American males no longer need to worry about appearing to act White or feminine if they do well in school. They should not have to make the agonizing choice of advanced classes or their friends. Why not have five African American males in honors classes together? The research shows that when Black students study together as a group, academic performance is improved. **Cooperative learning needs to be a cornerstone of our new and improved school culture.**[30]

Relevance

Black girls are often not motivated to pursue STEM careers because they see no relevance to their lives. So I asked Black girls how science, technology, engineering, and mathematics could become more interesting and attractive to them. What kinds of scientific experiments would they like to conduct? What kinds of research topics would they like to explore? The girls said they would like to study the following topics:

- Processed hair
- CPR
- STDs
- Pregnancy
- Delivering a baby
- Birth control
- Blood type
- Breast milk vs. cow's milk vs. formula
- Body fat, female to male
- Menstrual cycle
- HIV
- Asthma
- Smoking
- Marijuana
- Alcohol

Chapter Five: STEM

- Obesity
- Low birth rate
- Cancer
- Yeast infection
- Ear infection
- Crack
- Fibroid tumors
- Menopause
- Sickle cell anemia

Have you ever used any of these topics to motivate the girls in your science classes? These topics are just the tip of the iceberg. Our girls have a tremendous interest in math and science, but their interests are different than boys'. We must tailor our curriculum to their interests. Let us meet Black girls where they are. We need to make science come alive! Let's show them how their expertise in science could eventually reduce the cancer rate in the Black community. They could clean up air and water pollution in their neighborhoods.

Mentoring is extremely important in successful student development. Many books have been written on the positive impact mentoring can have on students. Mentoring can be extremely successful with Black girls. If we are going to increase the number of Black women in engineering and medicine, we must pair them with mentors from an early age.

In a subsequent chapter, we will revisit this in more detail, but here, I'd like to commend Spelman College and their outreach to several schools in the Atlanta area. Female college students are mentoring girls in elementary schools and high schools. I also want to commend Spelman's award winning robotics team.

I'd like to acknowledge FEMMES (Females Excelling More in Math, Engineering, and Science), Operation SMART, CODE, STEMBoard, and Million Women Mentors. These organizations are doing an excellent job, and I encourage readers to contact their local colleges, churches, community organizations, and businesses to identify Black women professionals in math and science who can mentor our girls. This is critical given the dearth of Black women teaching math and science.

Dedicate one day on a periodic basis to having STEM professionals and college students, specifically African American women, come in to speak to and encourage Black girls to pursue degrees and careers in STEM.

I'm excited to see an increase in the number of STEM charter schools, many of which are located in the heart of the inner city. We need to have single gender STEM charter schools in every city in America. Ideally, we should have as many single gender STEM charter schools as needed so that every Black girl who wants to pursue a STEM career would have a school that she could attend.

Every principal reading this book should identify Black female students—25 fifth graders and 25 ninth graders—to participate in a special STEM program. For the next four years, loop these girls with master teachers and incorporate the strategies that have been offered in this chapter. The goal is to give these students a quality STEM learning experience with master teachers who have bonded with them, have high expectations, understand their learning styles, and can master time on task. This is the least we should do. If we can't do it for all students, at least we can work with these deserving girls and show America that Black girls, if placed in the proper environment, can soar and excel in STEM!

Let me close with some good news. Earlier, I mentioned the work of Susan Goetz and her excellent book *Science for Girls*. When the strategies mentioned in this chapter are implemented, great things happen. Following are some successes she documents in her book.

- New York: The ratio of girls to boys in the computer lab used to be 2 to 25. Now it is 1 to 1.
- Wyoming: Girls' enrollment in physics rose from 56 percent to 62 percent, and in the

Introduction to Calculus course, enrollment rose from 45 percent to 71 percent.

- Oklahoma: The elective computer science class had no girls. It's presently at 31 percent.
- Nebraska: Precalculus enrollment, which had been 20 percent female, is now 45 percent female.
- West Virginia: The computer club used to be 5 percent girls. Now it's 53 percent girls.
- Montana: The computer programming class was 0 percent girls. Presently, it is 31 percent.
- Massachusetts: The science club is now 80 percent female. The math team is now 50 percent female; it was 20 percent.
- Colorado: 16 percent girls were in computer programming class. Presently, it is 30 percent.
- Arizona: Enrollment in upper-level math and science courses is up 18 percent.
- Virginia: The Advanced Placement class in physics was 0 percent. It is now 50 percent.
- Mississippi: The high school's math and science competitions were composed of seven boys and two girls. Presently, it is composed of seven girls and two boys.
- Oregon: The advanced math class rose from 37 percent female to 64 percent female.[31]

When we make math and science interesting, when we give girls confidence, when we have high expectations, when we make our pedagogy congruent with their learning styles, when we make STEM subjects relevant to Black girls, they soar, they strive!

I want to look at the brilliant scientist Eunice Cofie. Eunice grew up with low self-esteem. She has dark skin, and she was teased and bullied. She did not feel good about herself. Her father encouraged her to overcome these psychological hurdles and pursue science. Eunice fell in love with science, and she began to use her science skills to develop products that would enhance her beautiful, dark skin. Her self-esteem rose. Her science skills improved. She won numerous science fair competitions and tournaments and eventually created her own company, Nuekie, a cosmetics firm.

I wonder how many Eunice Cofies we have in Black America. How many Black girls do not feel good about their dark skin and the texture of their hair? Issues around natural hair, processed hair, and even synthetic weaves would be excellent to explore in research papers and science experiments.

I wonder: How many girls would fall in love with science if they could use science to address the issues that affect them?

I wonder: How many Black girls could use science to develop their own companies like Eunice Cofie has done with Nuekie?

In the next chapter, we will look at the importance of culture and *Her*story and the impact on Black girls.

Chapter Six: Herstory

The late great Maya Angelou said "I am the hopes and dreams of my ancestors".

I want to dedicate this chapter, to the four little girls, who were killed by the KKK, in the bombing of Sixteenth Street Baptist Church, on September 15, 1963 in Birmingham, AL.

Read the following questions, and write your answers in your notebook.

- What month does your school teach Black history?
- What month does your school teach White history?
- What month does your school teach women's history?
- What month does your school teach men's history?
- Why is Black history confined to the month of February, the shortest month of the year?
- Why is women's history confined to the month of March? Interestingly, Women's History Month was not signed into law until 1987.
- How many months during the year do we teach White male history?
- How many months do we teach Black female history?

Notice the title of this chapter: Herstory. History as it is traditionally taught is both racist and sexist. Schools teach much more about White history than Black history. They teach more about males than females. Listed below are five famous White and Black women. Can you match them based on their time and vocation in history?

White	Black
Susan B. Anthony	Madame C. J. Walker
Eleanor Roosevelt	Ida B. Wells
Harriet Beecher Stowe	Mary McLeod Bethune
Jane Austen	Harriet Tubman
Helena Rubinstein	Phillis Wheatley

Readers may have a difficult time juxtaposing an African American next to the White person. Could your Black female students match the above women? In this chapter, we want to emphasize the contributions of Black women. We want to learn about Black history and women's history all year long, not just in February and March. To help Black girls feel empowered, we must teach them to appreciate their history and culture.

More Q&A for your notebook:

- In your school, are Black girls taught their history and culture?
- Are they taught to recognize racism and sexism?
- Are they taught how to overcome and not accept racism and sexism?
- Can you name 20 famous Black women outside of sports and entertainment in history?
- Can you name 20 famous Black women outside of sports and entertainment presently?
- Can you name five African queens?
- Could the Black girls in your school answer the above questions successfully?

Your girls should be able to answer those questions. Ideally, your male students should be able to answer them as well. Here are a few more:

Chapter Six: Herstory

- Do you have any books in your classroom or school library that were written by Black women authors? Name ten.
- How visible are those books to your students?
- Are your students required to read the works of Black women writers?
- Are posters of Black women on the walls of your classroom and school? How visible are the posters?

In 1987, my company, African American Images, created a curriculum titled *SETCLAE—Self-Esteem Through Culture Leads to Academic Excellence.* This curriculum is now being used in more than 1,000 schools nationwide. It is a K–12 multicultural/Africentric curriculum. We believe that history and culture are the conduits to self-esteem and academic achievement. If you improve self-esteem, you improve academic achievement. The best way to enhance self-esteem is through history and culture. We believe that one month in February for Black history and one month in March for women's history are inadequate to achieve those goals.

- Have you ever heard your African American students tease each other for doing well academically and associate being smart with acting White?
- Have you ever heard White, Asian, or Jewish students tease each other for doing well academically and accuse each other of acting Black?
- Why is it that only African Americans associate being smart with other races? The answer lies in your school's curriculum.

African American students who know that Imhotep not Hippocrates was the father of medicine will never associate intelligence with being White. When children are ahistorical, apolitical, and acultural, they tend to make these asinine associations. In addition, if the curriculum fails to meet the cultural needs of Black girls, the following academic outcomes will probably occur:

- 82 percent below proficient in reading
- 87 percent below proficient in math
- 21 percent retained
- 40 percent dropped out
- 12 percent suspended
- 8 percent expelled
- 17.1 ACT college score
- 2 percent of the doctors

We can improve those figures by teaching Black girls their history and culture. Numerous schools using our SETCLAE curriculum have seen test scores improve from the 35th percentile to the 80th percentile and higher. There truly is a relationship between self-esteem and academic achievement. History and culture are the conduits.

How many schools are teaching African American students, specifically African American female students, their history and culture?

Black history and culture should be more than just names, dates, and events. In our textbook, *Lessons from History,* we move beyond names, dates, and events to address the deeper issues, such as:

- What were our historical strengths?
- What were our weaknesses?
- What can we learn from our history, and how can we apply those lessons to the present and future?

When I speak to Black students, one of the first things they tell me is that they are tired of talking about slavery. They want to know about their history before 1620. Do you know more Black history after 1620 or before? If you know more after 1620, then that's what you will probably teach to your students.

There is an historical law that says, *when* you start your history will determine *where* you will end up. If you start Black students in 1620, their beginning is on a plantation, and they will end up in a ghetto. If you start at 2780 B.C., they will start on a pyramid, and they'll end up being free. Where do you want to start

Black students in their history? Where do you want to start Black girls? On a plantation or a pyramid?

Again, I'd like to know if your school is doing anything special for Black girls. Some schools are dangerous to the psyches of Black females. These hostile environments are not nurturing or rewarding. It is heartbreaking to observe Black girls in some of these environments that I don't even want to call schools.

Jada Williams is a brilliant 13-year-old, eighth-grade student who attends School No. 3 in Rochester, New York. Her teacher told Jada and her classmates to read a book and write an essay about the book. Jada chose to read *The Narrative of the Life of Frederick Douglass.* She used the following quote in her essay: "If you teach that nigger how to read, there will be no keeping him. It would forever unfit him to be a slave. He would at once become unmanageable and of no value to his master."

Jada wrote that she was concerned about the poor reading performance of her peers in her school. Jada felt what Frederick Douglass experienced during slavery was taking place at her school. As a result of her brilliant analysis, Jada Williams was suspended and threatened with expulsion. Her case received national attention, and the Frederick Douglass Foundation awarded her a significant monetary prize. They felt she had fully internalized the legacy of Douglass.

- How would Jada Williams be received and accepted in your school?
- Are we encouraging African American students to be critical thinkers, even when their ideas may conflict with our own?
- Are we encouraging Black girls to read important African American books that have been critical of the Eurocentric ideal in American education and society?

What did Jada do wrong? She quoted Douglass' statement about slave owners being fearful of teaching slaves to read. A school like No. 3 in Rochester could break the spirit of a Jada Williams. It could affect her desire to pursue academic excellence and become a critical thinker. Our schools need to nurture and encourage students like Jada Williams. We need more Black female students like Jada Williams.

The next example comes from Precious Adams, an 18-year-old ballerina who hails from Detroit and is soon to become the first African American ballerina to complete an internationally renowned program at the Moscow State Academy of Choreography. While attending the ballet school, Precious faced persistent discrimination.

A group of young ladies would gather in a practice room waiting to be inspected and selected for parts in the Academy's anniversary celebration featuring superstars and ballet students from around the world.

A female instructor enters the room, looks the girls over, criticizing whether they are too heavy, too skinny or just not the right look. She steps to Precious and asked curtly, 'What are you doing here?' Then she asks her to leave the room. Although Precious has a pretty slender frame she doesn't look like the other students because she is black.

Precious is no stranger to being left out of shows because of the color of her skin. In fact, she had one instructor tell her to "try and rub the Black off" so that she could look more like the fairer, paler girls in her class.[32]

These are the kinds of experiences that many Black girls are having to endure.

- What is your school doing special for Black girls?
- How would Precious Adams be received in your school?
- Would Precious Adams be taught and encouraged to feel beautiful in your school?
- Would she be encouraged to reach her full potential?

I wonder how many young Black women like Precious Adams we have lost in hostile, negative, dangerous institutions that call themselves schools.

Chapter Six: Herstory

Carondelet High School in Concord, California, is a private high school with less than a 20 percent African American female population.[33] The administration decided that one month of Black history was too long, so they allocated just one day. Furthermore, rather than using the day to read Black authors and study Black history and culture, they decided to change the menu. Their way of celebrating Black History Month was to serve fried chicken, cornbread, and watermelon for lunch. They thought that was a more than adequate way of celebrating Black History Month.

Now really, how could they not know that was so wrong? To promote this Jim Crow stereotype, as if Whites never eat fried chicken, cornbread, and watermelon. How did they not know this was extremely offensive to their African American students? Are people really that naïve, or are we seeing racism rearing its ugly head yet again?

These are the kinds of environments and institutions that can destroy the psyche of African American females. I am constantly amazed at the resiliency of our girls in the face of tremendous odds.

Black Hair

In *Raising Black Girls,* there will be an entire chapter just on Black hair. Many times the term "good hair" is used. This is a dialectical term. If you know what good hair is, then you know what bad hair is. Unfortunately, for many Black girls living in White America and attending schools that are not nurturing to them, their hair does not meet White (and at times Black) approval.

Vanessa Vandyke is a 12-year-old honor roll student at Faith Christian Academy in Orlando, Florida. Vanessa liked to style her hair in beautiful puffs. She was suspended from school because her natural hair did not meet school approval.

How unfortunate that Vanessa and her family have to struggle with the school over her natural puffs. What kind of message are we sending to Vanessa? What is her school teaching her about her beauty and the texture of her hair?

Vanessa is not an isolated example. Tiana Parker is a seven-year-old honor roll student at Brown School in Tulsa, Oklahoma. She, too, was suspended from school because of her natural hair, which was styled in dreadlocks. The school felt that locks were not an appropriate style.

How is Tiana handling the experience of being embarrassed in front of her classmates at the young age of seven? What lesson will Tiana learn from this experience? To no longer wear dreadlocks or braids? To no longer wear her hair natural? That the only acceptable hair style in so-called schools is processed hair? Is that the message we want to give to Tiana and Vanessa?

But it doesn't stop there. An eight-year-old Black female student (name withheld) at Thurgood Marshall Elementary School in Seattle, Washington, was the only African American in her Accelerated Progress Program (APP) class. She was told by her White teacher to leave the class and stand outside the door because she did not like the smell of the moisturizer the student used in her hair. Notice, this school was named after Thurgood Marshall, the first African American justice to serve in the U.S. Supreme Court. I'm sure Thurgood Marshall is turning over in his grave at what's happening in this school named after him. As Charles Mudede, the student's father, wrote:

> If a white teacher—a person who is supposed to have a certain amount of education and knowledge of American history, and who teaches at a school named after the man who successfully argued before the court in *Brown v. Board of Education* for equal opportunities for racial minorities in public schools and went on to become the first African-American Supreme Court justice—removes a black student from a predominantly white class because of her hair, it is almost impossible not to read the action as either racist or expressive of racial insensitivity, which amounts to the same thing for someone in that teacher's position.[34]

Chapter Six: Herstory

Can you imagine the humiliation this child endured? All because a White teacher did not like the smell of the moisturizer that was used in her hair.

Black girls have been called the N-word and B-word, not just by their classmates, but by their *teachers*! Let it become mandatory in your school that all students and teachers review, critique, and write about the two movies, *Dark Girl* and *Good Hair* and *the speech given by Academy Award winning actress Lupita Nyong'o.*

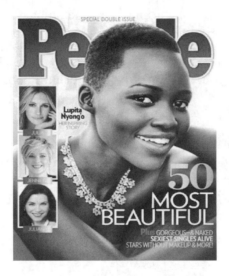

We need to have an open, honest discussion about hue and the beauty and benefits of dark skin and African hair texture. Many Black girls don't know about the benefits, and it's obvious that schools are not aware.

African queens. So what is Black Herstory, and how can we use Herstory to empower Black girls and help them improve their reading and math test scores, reduce retention, suspension, and dropout rates? One exciting example of Herstory are the stories of African queens. Your students can use the months of February and March and hopefully many more to study and write about them. They will learn about Black queens' rich history before 1620. They can create numerous engaging class projects around this subject. These are fascinating histories, and they will teach

Black girls about the inner strength, courage, scholarship, and leadership skills of these women. These queens were not B's and N's, and neither are Black girls. These African queens demanded respect. They were powerful and launched nation shaping movements.

Listed below are the names of some of the more well-known African queens. Have your students research, write about, critique, and appreciate these powerful women.

- Queen Hatshepsut – Egypt
- Queen Nefertiti – Egypt
- Queen Candace – Ethiopia
- Queen Nandi – Zulus of Southern Africa
- Queen Yaa Asantewaa – Ashanti Empire (modern day Ghana)
- Queen Nefertari – Egypt
- Queen Nzingah – Ndongo and Matamba Kingdoms (modern day Angola)
  Queen Makeda – Ethiopia
- Queen Tiye – Egypt
- Queen Cleopatra (Yes! Queen Cleopatra was Black!) – Egypt

Our girls need to learn about Black women before 1620. They need to know the history, beauty, and strength of Black women. What better place to start than with our queens?

Slavery.

Chapter Six: Herstory

Next we deal with slavery and beyond. In history you are taught about Black men being lynched. Did you know that hundreds of Black women were lynched during slavery? We need to expose Black girls and all students to The Mary Turner Project. While eight months pregnant, Mary Turner was publicly lynched. Black men weren't the only ones to suffer at the hands of racist White mobs. Black women were lynched, too. Have your girls study, write about, and show support for The Mary Turner Project. I also want all students, particularly Black female students to read about Maria Stewart and her powerful speech, "Why Sit Here and Die."

Sexism. When were White men given the opportunity to vote in America? 1776. When was it given to Black men? 1865. When was it given to women? 1920. Sexism during the Civil Rights Movement is yet another untold story. Did any African American women speak at Martin Luther King's March on Washington in 1963? Black women stood alongside Black men in the struggle for freedom during that important period in American history, but seldom is Herstory fully told. Our girls need to read, write about, and understand the work of Ella Baker, Fannie Lou Hamer, Jo Ann Robinson, Septima Clark, Oseola McCarty, and numerous others.

How was sexism portrayed in the Black Power Movement? Our girls need to read, write about, and understand the work of Angela Davis, Assata Shakur, Elaine Brown, Kathleen Cleaver, and numerous others.

How is sexism portrayed by gangsta rappers? Unfortunately, the many examples of sexism and misogyny in gangsta rap could fill volumes. Gangsta rap is dominated by young Black male artists and some aging MCs. These artists could have been celebrating and honoring our Black queens, our mothers, daughters, and sisters. Instead, some chose to promote a particularly cruel caricature of Black womanhood in their lyrics and music videos. Gangsta rap sexually objectifies and vilifies Black females both visually and lyrically. Gangsta rappers not only resurrected denigrating words used during slavery to describe Black females, they took it one step further and invented many of their own.

African American women consistently voiced their concerns over the years, and the women of Spelman College took a stand. Rap artist Nelly was scheduled to perform at a charity event on campus, but after the release of his notorious *Tip Drill* video—the one that depicted an African American female as an ATM machine—the students protested. As a result, Nelly cancelled his appearance. To this day he refuses to apologize or acknowledge their concerns.

I encourage Black females, under the supervision of educators, to watch the video, and more recent videos and review the lyrics, and then write about and discuss what the lyrics say about the state of Black womanhood and some men's perceptions of Black females.

How is sexism and racism portrayed in your school? We need to help and empower Black girls to recognize and overcome racism and sexism. Our girls need to be able to identify racist and sexist acts. They need to take a stand.

Earning Power
Why do Black women earn less than anyone else?

The Wage Gap by Gender and Race

White men	$100
White women	$80
Black men	$74
Black women	$69 [35]

Consider the following questions:
- Why do White men earn more than everyone else?
- Why do Black women earn $69 for every $100 White men earn?
- Why aren't White feminists outraged about Black women earning $69 to their $80?
- Why aren't Black men outraged that Black women earn $5 less than they do?

Chapter Six: Herstory

I encourage you to read "Other People's Daughters," the excellent article by Dr. Venus Evans-Winters and Jennifer Esposito.[36] Also, research the field of critical race feminism. The feminist movement has not been much concerned about the plight of Black females. This article and critical race feminism spotlight the intersection between racism and sexism.

Herstory in Education

Why don't we know much about the historical and cultural contributions of African American women? Our schools demonstrate little interest in teaching about the contributions of White females, much less Black females. During your next staff meeting, I'd like for you and your colleagues to discuss the following classic statements and questions which I've heard educators make over the years.

- I don't see color. I don't see race. I see children as children.
- I treat all students the same.
- How can the country be racist with a Black president?
- How is President Obama Black with a White mother?
- What is White privilege?
- I had nothing to do with racism or slavery. I am working two jobs and enrolled in school, trying to earn a better life.
- I don't believe people are suffering because of racism or sexism. I believe in the hard work ethic. Anyone can be successful in America if they work hard.
- How much wealth was earned by White Americans between 1620 and 1865? How was this wealth created?
- I don't understand why it's okay if Black kids use the N-word with each other, but it's not okay if White students or staff use the word.
- Why can't Blacks act like Asians and value academics and respect authority?

- A city has a $3 billion budget and 48 wards: 32 Black and Hispanic wards and 16 White wards. The 16 White wards receive two-thirds of the budget, but the new mayor wants each ward to receive $1/48^{th}$ of the $3 billion budget. Is that fair? How much will White wards lose, and how much will Black wards gain?
- What was the relationship between Thomas Jefferson and Sally Hemings?

Earlier, I asked you to name 20 famous Black females outside of sports and entertainment. Please study the list below and share with all your students.

- Harriet Tubman
- Ida B. Wells
- Rosa Parks
- Mary Church Terrell
- Mary Cary
- Crystal Fauset
- Mary Pleasant
- Winnie Mandela
- Barbara Sizemore
- Mary McLeod Bethune
- Ella Baker
- Madame C. J. Walker
- Carol Moseley Braun
- Marian Wright Edelman
- Michelle Obama
- Jo Ann Robinson
- Elaine Brown
- Condoleezza Rice
- Coretta Scott King
- Oseola McCarty
- Ellen Johnson Sirleaf (President of Liberia)
- Sojourner Truth
- Dorothy Height
- Fannie Lou Hamer
- Mary Bowser
- Bessie Coleman
- Frances Harper
- Maggie Walker
- Septima Clark
- Shirley Chisholm
- Angela Davis
- Oprah Winfrey
- Jocelyn Elders
- Maxine Waters
- Queen Mother Moore
- Barbara Jordan
- Assata Shakur
- Kathleen Cleaver
- Betty Shabazz
- Maria Stewart
- Catherine Samba-Panza (President of the Central African Republic)
- Joyce Banda (President of Malawi)

Chapter Six: Herstory

Readers, please add more to the list. I also encourage you to present the following list of Black women writers to your students. Does your school have books by these authors? Do you really want to empower Black female students?

- Sojourner Truth
- Nikki Giovanni
- Alice Walker
- Sharon Draper
- Toni Cade Bambara
- Gwendolyn Brooks
- Nannie Helen Burroughs
- Isabel Wilkerson
- Margaret Walker
- Pearl Cleage
- Paule Marshall
- J. California Cooper
- Sister Souljah
- Ntozake Shange
- Ida B. Wells
- Donna Marie Williams
- Venus Evans-Winters
- Jamaica Kincaid
- Iyanla Vanzant
- Monique Morris
- Paula Giddings
- Maya Angelou
- Sonia Sanchez
- Terry McMillan
- Toni Morrison
- Zora Neale Hurston
- Lorraine Hansberry
- bell hooks
- Patricia Hills Collins
- Octavia Butler
- Audre Lorde
- Rita Dove
- Kimberla Roby
- Beverly Sheftall
- Phillis Wheatley
- Harriet Jacobs
- Mary Lewis
- Dierdre Paul
- Joyce Ladner
- Melissa Harris-Perry
- Ruth Brown

I hope this chapter has helped you to appreciate how important it is to share Herstory and culture with your African American female students. We can improve the reading and math performance of Black girls. We can improve their test scores. We can reduce their retention, suspension, and dropout rates. All we have to do is simply teach girls to love themselves by teaching them their history and culture.

We could reduce suspensions and improve test scores if we taught Black females African values. Every girl should know the Nguzo Saba which are values celebrated during Kwanzaa and lived year round. They include: Unity, Self-Determination,

Collective Work and Responsibility, Cooperative Economics, Purpose, Creativity and Faith. They should also learn and internalize the values of Maat. They include Truth, Justice, Order, Harmony, Balance, Reciprocity and Righteousness. In the next chapter, we will look at the impact of Title IX and athletics on Black girls.

Chapter Seven: Athletics

One of the best days in the history of America was June 23, 1972. President Richard Nixon signed into law the statute known as Title IX, which declared, "No person in the United States shall, on the basis of sex, be excluded from participation in, be denied the benefits of, or be subjected to discrimination under any education program or activity receiving Federal financial assistance."

As a result of the passing of Title IX:

- In 1972, 3.7 million males and only 295,000 females participated in sports.
- Today, 3.2 million females and 4.5 million males are participating in sports.[37]

Even though Title IX has been in existence for more than 40 years, females still receive $183 million less in scholarships than their male counterparts. More work needs to be done to create a level playing field for females.

I am reminded of my own track career in high school and college. We won the city and state championship before Title IX. More than 75 females were cheerleaders for the track team. Many more joined the basketball, football, and baseball cheerleaders. All of those cheerleaders had the potential to be superior athletes in their own right.

Running track gave me the confidence to know, without a doubt, that I would graduate from high school and continue running track in college. I was motivated by my older classmates, many of whom continued their sport in college. I just assumed I would do the same. There are so many benefits of being involved in athletics, and we will discuss them throughout this chapter.

Girls have several sports from which to choose, and many girls are involved in more than one. Listed below are various sports and the representation of Black females in those sports.

Sport	Percent of Black Female Representation
Basketball	51
Track	28
Volleyball	12

Softball	8
Soccer	5
Lacrosse	1
Swimming	1
Tennis	1
Golf	1
Gymnastics	1
Ice skating	1 [38]

Q&A:

- Are Black girls better in basketball and track than White girls?
- Are White girls better than Black girls in lacrosse, swimming, tennis, golf, gymnastics, and ice skating?
- In track, are Black girls better in the 100-, 200-, and 400-meter races, the long jump, hurdles, high jumping, and triple jump? Are White girls better in the 800, 1500, 3000, 5000, 10,000, marathon and pole vaulting?
- Does racism exist in female athletics?
- Why is there a three times greater chance of receiving a scholarship in lacrosse, swimming, soccer, softball, volleyball, golf, tennis, ice skating, and gymnastics than in basketball and track?
- Where is the outcry from White feminists to get more Black girls involved in all sports?
- Are White feminists protecting some sports and scholarships for their daughters?
- Do predominately Black schools offer all sports to girls? Are Black girls exposed to opportunities to participate in all sports?

We could increase the number of Black females in college if we exposed them to lacrosse, swimming, soccer, softball, volleyball, golf, tennis, ice skating, gymnastics, and the longer track events.

In the NCAA Women's Basketball League, 51 percent of the athletes are Black females, but only 10 percent of the coaches are African American.[39] For some strange reason, White feminists are silent on this disparity.

I'm appealing to every high school in America to expose Black female students and encourage their participation in all

Chapter Seven: Athletics

sports. If they distinguish themselves in sports, an athletic scholarship could be their ticket to college.

I would now like to present an African American Female Athletes Hall of Fame:

- Basketball – Cynthia Cooper
- Track – Jackie Joyner-Kersee
- Lacrosse – Tina Sloan Green
- Swimming – Lia Neal
- Soccer – Briana Scurry
- Softball – Natasha Watley
- Volleyball – Flo Hyman
- Golf – Althea Gibson
- Tennis – Serena Williams
- Ice skating – Debi Thomas
- Gymnastics – Gabby Douglas
- Fencing – Nzingha Prescod
- Tae Kwon Do – Paige McPherson
- Bobsledding – Vonetta Flowers

Can you add four more names to each sport above? Have your students add more names. When African American women have the opportunity to participate in sports, *all* sports, they excel.

Have your Black female students read, write, discuss, and understand the tremendous work of Althea Gibson.

She dominated in two sports reserved for Whites: tennis and golf. Often compared to Jackie Robinson, the first African American to play in major league baseball, Althea was the first African American to play tennis on an international stage. She won the French Open in 1956 and Wimbledon in 1957 and 1958, among other tremendous feats.

Have your students write a letter to the mayor of New York, asking that the Arthur Ashe Stadium be renamed the Arthur Ashe-Althea Gibson Stadium. This woman was fantastic. She was brilliant, and she was courageous because she met and overcame racism at every turn. Every Black girl needs to read and appreciate the contributions of Althea Gibson.

Since the passage of Title IX in 1972, there has been a tremendous increase in the number of females participating in sports, from 295,000 to 3.2 million in 2014. Fifty-one percent of White female students participate in at least one sport compared to only 40 percent of Black females.[40] How can we make sports attractive to the other 60 percent?

There are several reasons for the lack of participation.

1. *Hair.* One-third of Black girls who do not play a sport give hair maintenance as the major reason for their lack of participation. (Interestingly, according to the *Archives of Dermatology*, 40 percent of adult African American women don't exercise for the same reason.[41]) If the definition of good hair is long, straight, processed, and permed, if you can be suspended, sent to the corner, sent outside the classroom, and expelled and removed from the military because of your natural, textured hair, then nonparticipation, while unfortunate, makes sense. They don't want their hair to "go back."

2. *Boys.* Being involved in sports means that females will have demanding academic, practice, and competition schedules. That means they can't hang out with their boyfriends. Also, many Black girls think they are unattractive when they are practicing and competing. They may worry about becoming "too dark" if they have to work out in the sun, or they worry about their hair (see #1 above).

3. *Body consciousness.* Some girls' uniforms (e.g., volleyball) are far too revealing for comfort. Believe it or

not and contrary to media depictions, Black girls can be very modest in their attire. Not all are trying to put their bodies on display for the world to see. Coaches and gym teachers must become more sensitive to the developmental, psychological, and social issues girls have with their changing bodies. Girls of all sizes say they sometimes refuse to take gym class or try out for a sport because the uniforms are too tight or reveal too much skin. One mother told me her daughter had straight As in all her eighth grade classes—except gym. She got a D in gym because she refused to take the class; the mother believed her daughter felt highly self-conscious in the gym uniform. As a result, she was passed over for class valedictorian. Girls say that even if they are wearing jeans, their gym teachers won't let them participate in class because of the uniform policy. I can understand the need to wear sneakers, but why be so dogmatic about a rule that can make girls feel uncomfortable in their own skins? Maybe the rule needs to be revisited.

4.   *Obesity.* According to the U.S. Office of Minority Health, African American women and their daughters have the highest rates of being overweight or obese compared to other groups in the country.[42] Physical activity is just about the best remedy for obesity; however, if our girls are made to wear shorts and school-issued tops that don't fit well, many will opt out of gym and sports altogether. It can be embarrassing for some overweight girls to even *order* a gym uniform, much less wear one that shows too much skin or is too tight. Especially in middle school and high school, girls are acutely and painfully aware of how their bodies look in comparison to other girls' bodies. They are constantly judging themselves in comparison to other girls, and this is true of most girls, regardless of size or race. Overweight Black girls attending Black schools fare better than if they attend White schools. This is a complex issue for Black girls, and complicating matters, our society has taught them to be hyper critical of and sexualize every body part. Today there is a movement to help overweight women and girls love their bodies, even as they're attempting to get healthy. Still, given hostile school environments and uniform rules that fail to consider

103

developmental and self-esteem issues, our girls may choose to pass on athletics altogether.

5. *Co-ed gym.* Co-ed gym class can be one of the most harrowing periods of the day for many girls. When I was growing up, gym classes were usually single gender. Today, many gym classes are mostly co-ed. Given the requirement to wear gym shorts, swim suits, etc., it's no wonder that some girls cut this class. Another issue is that girls don't want to appear uncoordinated in front of boys. They don't want to be teased. It's the job of gym teachers and coaches to provide heavy doses of encouragement and motivation to girls who are insecure about their athletic performance. Unfortunately, in many inner city schools, gym is only offered once a week. I have consulted in some high schools where it's only required for one year.

6. *Lack of school support.* Many schools have not encouraged Black girls to be involved in sports, especially in those sports that seem to be reserved for White girls. One way to address this issue is to have a weeklong sports fest for girls. Create stations and feature a sport at each. Girls are encouraged to visit each station to feel and handle, for example, golf clubs, lacrosse sticks, tennis rackets, softballs, swords, etc. Have sign-up sheets for tryouts at every station. Each girl must sign up for one sport.

7. *Lack of transportation.* Many girls don't participate in sports because of the logistics between home and school. Many inner city schools do not offer transportation. Taking public transportation after practice can be dangerous in some communities. Often our girls don't feel safe going home by themselves in the dark.

8. *Lack of parental support.* Many girls say their parents do not encourage them to become involved in sports because they are needed at home to take care of younger siblings. Parents make athletics a priority for sons, but not daughters. I recommend offering workshops to educate parents about the tremendous benefits athletics has for girls, including the following:

    - There's a 25 percent less chance of students dropping out of school if they are involved in sports.
    - The field of athletics improves GPA. Researchers at Michigan State University determined that students

who participated in sports did 10 percent better in science, English, math and social studies compared to other students.

- Participation in sports increases girls' interest in pursuing STEM careers. The brilliant African American figure skater Debi Thomas won a bronze medal in the 1988 Olympics, and later she went on to become an orthopedic surgeon. Remember, only two percent of doctors in this country are African American females. If athletics increases girls' interest in STEM careers, then we should do everything we can to encourage their participation in sports.

Just because you didn't start out perfect doesn't mean you can't have an excellent result in the end.

Debi Thomas
www.carolcolmancollages.com

- Participation in sports develops leadership skills. Sports could help reduce the suspension rate, which is at 12 percent for Black girls.
- Participation in sports increases the chance of Black girls attending and graduating from college. This would reduce the 40 percent high school dropout rate.
- Participation in sports lowers the rate of sexual activity, and consequently, STDs and out-of-wedlock pregnancies.
- There's a 29 percent less chance of becoming a smoker if you participate in sports. Fifteen percent of Black women are smokers, and 10 percent of pregnant females smoke.
- There is less chance of being obese and overweight if girls are involved in athletics. First Lady Michelle Obama has done a tremendous job of trying to get everyone, especially girls, to get on the move.
- There is less chance of breast cancer. Presently, 30,000 African American women die annually of cancer. Black females have a 41 percent higher death rate than White women. Again, the White feminist community has been silent on this disparity. We could reduce the incidence of cancer in the Black female community if we had more girls and women participating in sports.
- When Black girls are involved in sports, they have a greater participation in the workforce, and they receive higher wages. They also develop the leadership skills to become entrepreneurs.[43]

We need to have an all-out blitz to get the 60 percent of Black girls who are not participating in sports involved. The benefits are just too great to overlook.

I want to conclude this chapter by honoring Jaelyn Bates and Winifred Pristell.

Chapter Seven: Athletics

Jaelyn plays on the boys fourth-grade basketball team at Frey Academy because the girls did not give her enough competition. She is also one of the best players on the boys' team. Her team was denied participation in a state tournament because of her gender. The coach, the boys, parents and the entire school wanted their star player to remain to give them an opportunity to win. It has now gone into litigation. There are hundreds of females like Jaelyn on boys' sports teams, performing exceptionally.

Winifred Pristell is the reigning weight lifting champion. Amazingly she is a 75-year-old great-grandmother. She was suffering with arthritis and was almost immobile. She remembered how much she enjoyed athletics when she was younger and returned to her favorite sport and regained her health.

In the next chapter, we will look at the educational challenges facing Black girls.

Chapter Eight: Educational Challenges

	Female	Male
Reading (below proficient)	82 percent	90 percent
Math (below proficient)	88 percent	88 percent
ACT	17.1	16.8
Retention	21 percent	29 percent
Suspension	12 percent	24 percent
Expulsion	8 percent	15 percent
Dropout rate	40 percent	47 percent

If 82 percent of White females were below proficient in reading, America would declare a state of emergency. If 88 percent of White girls were below proficient in math, this would be considered a major crisis in America. If 21 percent of White girls were retained, there would be a major outcry. If White girls only scored 17.1 on the ACT, there would be national conferences to discuss the problem. If 40 percent of White girls dropped out, it would be a catastrophe. If 12 percent of White girls were suspended and 8 percent expelled, it would make national news. Where is the outrage from the feminist community, the Black community, and the educational community regarding the plight of Black girls? Black boys are on life support, Black girls are in critical condition, and we do not need to ignore one to address the other. This is not an either/or issue. Both groups need help. For too long, Black girls have been denied the assistance they have needed because of the tremendous challenges and conditions facing African American males.

School Culture

Educators tend to subscribe to the idea that race, income, number of parents in the home, educational background of parents, parental involvement in school, and the level of school funding are the sole determinants of academic performance. When parents are single, Black or Hispanic, low-income, and non-degreed, teachers assume the students will not do well. Their expectations are low.

However, in my book *There Is Nothing Wrong with Black Students*, I (with assistance from Education Trust, the National Center of Educational Accountability, and the National Center for School Transformation) identified *hundreds* of schools located in high-risk communities where students scored well above the national average on standardized tests. Risks may exist in homes and communities, but these successful schools prove that students can excel academically regardless of the circumstances.

When I first visit a school, I review the academic performance and behavioral issues of Black students. In addition and perhaps even more important than the raw data, I try to get a feeling for the school's culture, because school culture will tell me nearly everything I need to know about why Black students are performing and behaving in certain ways. So I walk the halls, visit classrooms, and talk to students and teachers. I observe how teachers and Black students in particular relate and communicate. Is your school's culture hospitable or hostile to Black girls? Listed below are some of the ways I assess school culture.

School name. I can tell an awful lot about a school by ascertaining if the students know anything about the individual after whom the school is named. Can you imagine a school being named after Frederick Douglass, yet the students never read anything about him? They may not know that it was illegal for slaves to learn how to read, but Douglass would still sneak away every evening to read. As a result, he was beaten on a regular basis. We mentioned earlier that Jada Willams wrote a brilliant essay on Douglass; she could have attended a school named after Douglass and helped her peers and teachers understand his contributions. It's just amazing the number of students and teachers who are clueless about the major contributions made by the namesakes of their schools.

Posters. I believe a picture is truly worth a thousand words. What the educators have decided to place on the walls lets me know what they think of our students, particularly Black girls. What do your posters say about your perceptions of Black girls?

Teachers' lounge. I often visit the teachers' lounge (incognito). This is a good way to listen to conversations teachers have among themselves. In low-achieving schools, the conversations are full of negativity. Students and parents should never hear what's being said about them because they would be angry and devastated. What do the teachers talk about in your teachers' lounge? Are teachers discussing ways to help their African American female students, or are they grunting and griping about girls with attitude? Are teachers primarily sharing their frustrations with one another, or are they sharing the latest research?

Chapter Eight: Educational Challenges

How can you make your teachers' lounge a more inspiring, productive place to visit?

Low-Achieving vs. High-Achieving Schools

Teachers are the key to creating school culture. A school can have a positive culture, where both teachers and students are engaged and learning is fun. Negative school cultures, on the other hand, foster low efficacy among teachers and poor academic performance among students.

In low-achieving schools, teachers don't really believe the students can learn. Their expectations are low, and as a result, too many of our girls are performing below their ability. These teachers may say, "All students can learn," but they rarely say, "All students *will* learn." In the next chapter, we will look at schools that believe all students *will* learn. There's a tremendous difference between *can* and *will*. *Can* refers to the innate, often unrealized intellectual ability of students, while *will* implies the energetic, determined participation of teachers in ensuring student achievement.

In low-achieving schools, good teachers are not celebrated. Bad teachers are allowed to remain and infect the culture. Let's say there are two teachers: one produces excellent outcomes in students while students of the other teacher are performing far below average. When cuts to the budget must be made, the inferior teacher is allowed to remain because of seniority while the newer high-achieving teacher is removed.

In low-achieving schools, it's unions first. In high-achieving schools, it's children first. Educators say they are in it for the children, but most educational decisions are not made in the best interest of children. Remember, education is political and most educators are politicians. Tracking is better for teachers, not for children. Departmentalization is better for teachers, not students. Teaching 30 children with one pedagogy is better for teachers, not children. Removing a high-achieving teacher with low seniority is better for unions, not children. Placing a disproportionate number of Black children in special education is beneficial for teachers not students. Funding schools based on property taxes is better for middle-income and high-income families, not for children—especially children of color who come from low-income families.

When visiting a school, I take note of how soon the staff exit the school at the end of the day. In low-achieving schools, the staff literally leaves at the same time as the students. In high-achieving schools, the staff may leave 15, 30, 45 minutes, even an hour later as they review their lesson plans, prepare for tomorrow's class, and collaborate with their peers to improve their craft.

Race and Gender of Faculty and Staff
Following are questions to explore in your notebook:
- What is the racial makeup of your students? What is the racial make-up of your faculty? What is the racial makeup of your non-teaching staff?
- What is the gender make-up of your students? What is the gender make-up of your faculty? What is the gender make-up of your non-teaching staff?
- What are the chances of your Black female students experiencing a STEM class taught by an African American woman?
- What message are we sending to children when 80 percent or more of the faculty are White and 80 percent of the non-teaching staff are adults of color?
- What is your school doing to increase the percentage of teachers of color?
- What is your school doing to increase the percentage of Black females teaching a STEM class?
  Let's take another look at the performance of Black females:
  - 82 percent below proficient in reading
  - 87 percent below proficient in math
  - 21 percent retained
  - ACT test scores, 17.1
  - 40 percent dropout
  - 12 percent suspended
  - 8 percent expelled
  - 2 percent of the doctors

Low-achieving schools use tests solely for evaluation purposes. They consolidate 180 days of lessons to four or five days of testing. The state exam is given, let's say, in March. Despite our high tech age, it takes some schools almost two months to receive the test scores. So the test was given in March, and the results are not returned until May, and the school year ends late May, early June. But even if we're restricted to using test results for evaluation purposes in May, we can still disaggregate the scores

Chapter Eight: Educational Challenges

in August or September to pinpoint areas of difficulty in reading and math. For example, are problems in reading caused by a vocabulary deficiency? Is the problem comprehension? Fluency? Phonics? Writing? What's causing the low scores in math? Basic math operations, word problems, multiplication tables, decimals, fractions, or percentages? Once assessed, these issues will be addressed in the upcoming school year with each student. In the next chapter, we'll discuss this idea further.

In high-achieving schools, teachers create almost a war room. They review the test data, and that drives the pedagogy and curriculum for the next cycle. If we want to improve the academic performance of Black girls, we must use the state exam and Common Core results for diagnostic purposes, and we must do this throughout the year.

Suspensions/Expulsions
Q&A:
- Twelve percent of Black girls are suspended and 8 percent are expelled. Black girls are suspended or expelled four times more than White girls. How do we explain this disparity?
- In your school, are Black girls and White girls treated the same?
- Are White girls warned and Black girls suspended or expelled?
- If there is a violation of the uniform policy, are White girls warned and Black girls suspended or expelled?
- If White girls are using their mobile device, are they warned? If Black girls do the same are they suspended or expelled?
- If a White girl and a Black girl are both chewing gum, is the White girl warned while the Black girl is suspended or expelled?
- Are Black girls suspended or expelled in your school because they are different than White girls?
- Are Black girls suspended or expelled in your school because they are louder than White girls?
- Are Black girls suspended or expelled because they roll their eyes at you? Because they move their neck? Because they put their hands on their hips and say, "Whatever"?

- Are Black girls suspended or expelled because they have too much attitude? Because they're too sassy?
- Some girls like Jada Williams are suspended because they are critical thinkers and Africentric.
- One girl was suspended because she did not like her teacher calling her retarded.
- A three-year-old girl was expelled from preschool for using a word of profanity. The parent said the child had not heard the word from home nor did her daughter understand the word.
- White girls receive counseling and Black girls are expelled.
- Are Black girls suspended or expelled for questioning the teacher?

Harmani Osbi is a beautiful seven-year-old special needs child attending Cohen School in Philadelphia. She was chewing her sweater to the disdain of her special education teacher. The educator forcefully removed the sweater and in the process pulled out three of Harmani's teeth.

Samaya Dillard is another beautiful seven-year-old student attending Jefferson School in Sacramento. She tried her best to please her teacher, to no avail. The teacher always made disparaging comments about Samaya publicly. One day the teacher removed her from the class and left her in the hallway for over an hour. Samaya felt so bad she left the school and proceeded to walk to the highway to kill herself. Fortunately, she was rescued.

In many schools, the psyche of Black girls is being destroyed.

I encourage you to read the excellent article by Edward Morris, "'Ladies' or 'Loudies'?"[44] He cites instances when some teachers perceive Black females as being loud, assertive, sassy, confrontational, defiant, challenging, and not respecting authority. In many schools, quiet girls are overlooked and loud girls are punished. Some teachers question your womanhood if you are loud and tell them to be quiet and act like a lady. Morris mentions that one school created a Proper Ladies Club to teach Black girls to be quiet, unassertive, compliant, compromising, and respectful of authority figures regardless of what they say. Morris indicates that many of the qualities that made these female students academically sound were being destroyed with this club. This reminds me of the "Seasoning" process that plantation owners used during slavery to break the African spirit. In the book *Roots*, it amounts to converting Kunte Kinte into Toby. Is your school trying to break the spirit of Black girls? Is your school trying to convert Aisha to Annie?

The Department of Education's Office for Civil Rights documented that White and Black students were involved in identical behavior, but Black students were punished more harshly. If it was a first time offense, Black students had a 200 percent greater chance of being suspended. If they were suspended Black students had a 300 percent greater chance for their suspension to be outside of school while White students received in-school suspension. While the national suspension average is 12 percent, Michigan and Missouri are 16 percent and Wisconsin is 21 percent. Females with disabilities have a 19 percent propensity of suspension.[45]

Is your school fair to Black girls? Are they given another chance? Can their suspension be served inside the school?

Many Black girls are torn between the dichotomy of good girl and ghetto girl. They want to be good, but they live in neighborhoods where survival is paramount. They know that schools prohibit fighting, but their peer group requires self-defense. They know they should tell their teachers if they are bullied, but they also know most teachers will not protect them. I encourage staff members to read the seminal work of Elijah Anderson, *Streetwise*.[46] He describes the three salient factors for youth: reputation, respect and retaliation. Educators must appreciate these three variables and help girls keep their reputation and respect without retaliation. If schools do not teach this skill, girls will retaliate and face suspension. I encourage schools to identify 25 girls who are prone to retaliating and provide them with counseling, mentoring, and rites of passage.

I recommend that schools become proactive and address the root issue driving so many girls to fight. Violence is an expression of powerlessness. When Black girls have not been nurtured and mentored by teachers, when they have not been made to feel beautiful, when their natural hair is not revered; when they are not respected and valued, when no one listens, when the curriculum does not include their history and culture, when their attitude and volume are not appreciated, they will lash out in anger at their peers. In my next book for parents, we will explore this issue in more detail. In the following chapter on solutions we will also address this issue.

I also encourage you to read the excellent work being done by Monique Morris at the National Black Women's Justice Institute. She describes in detail the school to jailhouse pipeline for Black females. They are 31 percent of the girls referred by schools to law enforcement and are 43 percent of females with a school-related arrest. If placed in residential placement, they have a 42 percent chance of suffering physical abuse.[47]

Teachers will often tell Black girls to "Get rid of the attitude." Ironically, a fashion director will say to a model, "Give me some attitude!"

Do we have double standards? When White girls have attitude we call it "strong leadership potential," but when Black girls have strong leadership potential we say they have "too much attitude."

- Does your school encourage and appreciate Black female attitude?
- Does your school feel like a school or a prison?
- In your school, are students given a second or third chance?
- Is zero tolerance the mindset and rule of the day?
- Do girls act like boys? Do Black girls act like boys?
- Do girls dress like boys? Do Black girls dress like boys?
- Is your school's uniform policy sensitive to the female physique?
- Is there any difference between your school's uniforms and prison uniforms?
- Eighty-one percent of girls report they have been bullied in school. Is your school safe for girls? Is it safe for Black girls?

Why do so many girls fight over boys? I was disheartened to read that an 11-year-old girl died in school fighting over a boy. Two 14-year-old girls got into an argument over a boy on Facebook and one killed the other. Have you noticed the differences between girls and boys as it relates to fighting? Boys can fight and then have lunch with each other the next hour. When girls fight, most can keep it going for the rest of the school year. When boys fight, it's usually about money or some valued possession. When girls fight it's usually over something petty, something that was said, something that was written in Facebook or Twitter, a text, or an email.

Improving academic performance will be difficult if 12 percent of your students are not in school because of suspensions and are expelled. We must also look at the fact that 20 percent of teachers (referral agents) are making 80 percent of the referrals for suspension.[48] In the next chapter, we will look at what schools have done to address the 20 percent. The problem may not be with Black girls. It may be the school's culture. It may be the Referral Agent/teacher's inability to manage her class well. It may be the unfairness between how Black girls and White girls are treated. It may be that we have not appreciated Black girls or understood their attitudes. Maybe Black girls are not bossy. Maybe they're leaders. As Beyoncé says, "I'm not bossy / I'm the boss."

Schools could reduce female suspensions if they gave more respect to Black females. Schools could reduce female suspensions if they protected them better from negative male behavior. If the teacher heard the boy call her a derogatory name and touch her private parts why should the female have to "snitch" on the male? Most fights between females are a result of low self-esteem, colorism, and hair texture.

We need to celebrate Black girls and their strengths, not suspend them.

Dropout Rate

Forty percent of Black girls drop out. Many Black girls don't drop out, they are pushed out or expelled. They are pushed out by schools that never taught them reading or math. They are pushed out by schools that don't like their hair, attitude and Africentric values. They are pushed out because they were suspended for over 20 days outside of school. What is your school doing to help Black girls stay in school? How you answer that question will determine your success and efficacy in reducing the dropout rate.

If your school is doing special things for Black girls, then they will want to stay in school. Some schools are so hostile, drab, and sterile that staff doesn't want to be there any more than the students. They are discouraged from attending. In fact, we see

Black girls dropping out in high school, but in reality, the seeds of their exodus began emotionally in fourth grade.

Black girls who drop out say they know they aren't missed by their former teachers. No one from school called to find out why they weren't there. They simply walked away from each other, no questions asked. Does that happen in your school? Can students just drop out and not be missed?

There are at least four school-based risk factors that may lead to dropping out: low attendance, test scores below proficiency, high retention, and suspensions. If we're serious about reducing the dropout rate of Black girls, the first order of business in your war room is to create an effective strategy to improve school attendance. Focus special attention on Black girls whose attendance rates are below 90 percent.

Teen Pregnancy
One of every ten Black girls will give birth to a child before their 20th birthday. With the dropout rate at 40 percent, the last thing we want is for Black girls to get pregnant.

How schools address teen pregnancy is a highly controversial issue. For example, some schools have "baby days," where the teen mothers bring their babies to school and are glorified for giving birth while in high school. Without a doubt, schools providing child care, counseling, and the option to do school work at home during the last month or two of pregnancy have helped to reduce the dropout rate. However, I wonder if the "baby day" schools also have academic and athletic assemblies for Black girls who are achieving. We send the wrong message when we honor the mistake and neglect the achievement.

Learning Styles
Not all girls learn the same way. Boys and girls are different. They have different learning styles. This does not mean that all boys are left brain learners and all girls are right brain learners. This does not mean that all boys prefer math and science and all girls prefer language arts. There are at least five different learning styles: written, oral, visual, tactile, and kinesthetic. Black girls who are below proficient in reading and math could improve their test scores and classroom performance if teachers would change their pedagogy to meet Black girls' learning styles.

Chapter Eight: Educational Challenges

Take a moment to consider the learning styles of your Black female students. On a sheet of paper, write down each student's name. Next to each name, write whether you think her primary learning style is written, oral, visual, tactile, or kinesthetic. Many schools expect students to learn in only one modality: written. Believe it or not, some girls are tactile and kinesthetic learners. Not every Black girl is going to master concepts via textbooks and worksheets. We need to allow for the fact that students have different learning styles.

One reason why Black girls are scoring 82 percent below proficient in reading and 87 percent below in math is because their teachers only use textbooks and worksheets in the classroom. See if you can go one day a week without using a textbook or worksheet. Try going one day a week without lecturing. Don't think you can correct the problem by simply playing a video for 45 minutes and think that is a lesson. Granted, many Black girls are visual learners, but they need to do more than sit in front of a video for 45 minutes.

Some girls need more movement, just like some boys; these are your kinesthetic learners. Your tactile learners require more hands-on activities. Not every girl has a long attention span. Not every girl likes working quietly by herself for long periods of time on a worksheet. We need to allow for a wide variety of learning styles.

I suggest one day a week, we allow code or culture switching. We allow them to speak Ebonics. I also suggest on this day they can respond without raising their hand. I have also noticed that teachers prefer only one response at a time. This is designed for the teacher to hear what is being said because students have no problem hearing several voices and following numerous conversations in progress. Many Black girls have been called rude and suspended because they spoke Ebonics, did not raise their hands before responding, and spoke while other students were commenting.

Attitude

Not all girls are passive. Not all girls have a desire to please the teacher. Black girls are not White girls. Many Black girls are talkative and confrontational. These same Black girls may have honor roll and leadership potential. They could become the next Condoleezza Rice, Mae Jemison, Michelle Obama, or

Maxine Waters. Unfortunately, because they have been misdiagnosed, they are being labeled as negative and attitudinal. Many teachers want Black girls to get rid of what could be their greatest strength, their attitude. Instead, as you attempt to understand, appreciate, and like Black girls, try encouraging them to give *more* attitude.

Our girls need to be valued for who they are, and they surely should not be compared to White girls.

Does your school allow Black girls to be unique? To be themselves?

How can their attitude be used to improve test scores, GPA, and leadership abilities?

In the next chapter, we will provide more educational strategies to help Black girls.

Chapter Nine: Educational Solutions

1. The principal serves as the instructional leader.
2. School culture is optimistic.
3. All students *will* learn.
4. Implement a Teacher of the Month program.
5. Reduce or remove ineffective teachers.
6. Increase African American female teachers.
7. Increase African American female teachers in STEM subjects.
8. Train all teachers in Teacher Expectations Student Achievement (TESA).
9. Address and abolish racism and sexism in your school.
10. Like, respect, culturally understand, and love Black girls.
11. Loop master teachers.
12. Place the best teachers in the primary grades.
13. Hold a monthly book club featuring books by Black women writers.
14. Purchase Best Books for Girls from African American Images.
15. Hold monthly math and vocabulary contests.
16. Use tests for diagnostic purposes.
17. Employ greater use of phonics.
18. Study and implement the Singapore Math model.
19. Abolish social promotion.
20. Only allow in-house school suspensions.
21. Abolish zero tolerance.
22. Require 100 percent approval of suspensions from the local school committee.
23. Increase your classroom's time on task.
24. Hold a Black Girls Rock monthly convocation.
25. Take Black girls on a monthly field trip.
26. Implement a peer mentoring program.
27. Implement an adult mentoring program.
28. Implement a rites of passage program.
29. Have Black girls learn and play chess.
30. Make sure that a retained student gets a different teacher, pedagogy, curriculum, greater time on task, single gender class and/or single gender cooperative learning group.
31. Use SETCLAE curriculum for the school year, not just in February.

32. Hang posters of African American women throughout the school.
33. Hang the "Phenomenal Woman" poster throughout the school.
34. Implement a single gender model in cooperative learning groups, math and science classes.
35. Teach Black girls the psychology of performance
36. Implement a STEM program for primary grades.
37. Implement a STEM program for intermediate grades.
38. Implement a STEM program for high school.
39. Increase the percentage of girls in athletics, expose them to all sports, and include cross-subject coverage of sports (such as history, math, writing, and science).
40. Appreciate the attitudes of Black females.
41. Do not compare Black females to White females.
42. Appreciate Black hairstyles.
43. Provide lesson plans for all learners: written, oral, visual, tactile, and kinesthetic.
44. Have colleges, businesses, and churches adopt your school.
45. Create a war room dedicated to working with Black girls who are at risk of dropping out. Identify Black girls with suspensions, low attendance, and poor test scores to participate.
46. Install drop boxes throughout the school to encourage Black girls to voice their concerns.
47. Principals should host quarterly pizza parties for Black female honor roll students, those with the greatest academic improvement and those participating in STEM competitions.
48. If the student has not learned the teacher has not taught.

Let's now review some the above solutions in more detail.

Principals
There are two types of principals in America: CEOs and instructional leaders. CEOs love their offices. They spend most of their time in the office. They prefer being the school's accountant or building manager. They spend little time outside their offices.

Instructional leaders, on the other hand, spend very little time in their offices. Most of the day they can be found walking the corridors, monitoring students, and visiting classrooms. CEOs only visit classrooms once a year for the evaluation. Instructional leaders are in classrooms on a regular basis, and teachers encourage principals' input and advice. CEOs do not make positive changes to school culture. Only instructional leaders can do that.

Chapter Nine: Educational Solutions

Successfully educating Black girls begins and ends with the principal.

High-achieving schools have an optimistic school culture. They believe their children *will* learn, and they will learn this year. They believe that in spite of the external factors that are taking place in the home and larger community, they can make a difference. Their efficacy is high.

It is very difficult for teachers to change the school's culture if the principal is not on board. The tragedy is that too many principals overseeing schools in at-risk communities subscribe to the deficit model of students' ability to learn. Given what's occurring in the home and larger community, they do not believe they can make a difference. As a result, they burn out and quit. Too many of our children attend schools that have had four principals in four years, and all were CEOs. I hold superintendents personally responsible for these poor personnel decisions and allowing this systemic problem to fester to the detriment of students and teachers.

In high-achieving schools, instructional leaders stay late, and their enthusiasm and commitment are contagious. Teachers in these schools elect to stay after hours as well. There's such a warm and encouraging atmosphere in these schools. The teachers' lounge is an exciting place where ideas are shared, research is disseminated, and teachers are inspiring one another to succeed. They positively hold each other accountable.

Nationwide, African American students are 18 percent of students, but only six percent of teachers are African American, and only five percent are African American women. Successfully educating Black girls means we must increase the percentage of Black women teachers.

Let me share with you some very interesting scholarship that ironically comes from a White professor, Thomas Dee of Swarthmore College. His article is titled "Teacher's Race and Student Achievement in Randomized Experiment."[49]

I want to also share research from the article, "Minority Teachers Reduce African-American Teen Pregnancy Rate."

African American teachers drive down African American teenage pregnancy rates. Looking at Georgia Public School data from 143 districts, comparing teacher representation in high schools and teen pregnancy rates reported by districts to the Georgia Department of Community Health, they found that increasing the number of minority teachers decreases teen pregnancy among those populations. You do not see a decrease in teen pregnancy for African American teenagers until you reach a critical mass of African American teacher representation. We identified 17.6 percent as the tipping point where the percentage of African American teachers started to significantly lower the African American teen pregnancy rate. Study findings show a 10 percent increase in African American teachers will result in six fewer African American teen pregnancies per district. Districts with 20 to 29 percent African American teachers resulted in a significant decrease in teen pregnancies: 18.8 fewer pregnancies per 1,000 students.[50]

Since 1954, there has been a 66 percent decline in African American teachers.[51] Historically, Black teachers taught longer and were more of a surrogate parent. Presently, 40 percent of teachers leave within five years.[52] Eighty-three percent of America's elementary school teachers are White and female.[53] I am now spending almost three days a week primarily working with White female teachers. Is the future of the Black race, specifically Black girls, in the hands of White female teachers?

In my book, *Black Students, Middle Class Teachers,* I said that it may not be just the race or gender of the teacher that makes the difference in the classroom. It's the teacher's expectations, time on task, and their ability to be fair with students. I point out that there are some "Negro" teachers who are dangerous. They do not like, respect, culturally understand, or love African American children. There are some White teachers, including White *male* teachers, who may have a greater bond with Black female students than a Black woman teacher. Until the demographics change, we will have to work with the teachers we have. I'm imploring all White teachers, especially White female teachers, to not be afraid of Black girls, to appreciate their attitudes. **Don't compare Black girls to White girls.** I implore you to like, respect, understand, and love Black girls. If you can't do that, then you need to honestly ask yourself why you're teaching in this school.

Chapter Nine: Educational Solutions

Abolish Racism and Sexism

This is a monumental task. First, we're addressing the elephant in the room. Most people, and educators are no different, do not want to talk about racism or sexism. They especially do not want to acknowledge that they could be racist and/or sexist. Few people want to talk about White privilege. Our society and particularly schools could learn from the NBA and how quickly they addressed racism shown by the Los Angeles Clippers' owner Donald Sterling. It is even more difficult for me, an African American consultant, to discuss racism and sexism with a predominately White staff. They would feel uncomfortable discussing race and gender issues with a White consultant, but I'm sure my race complicates matters for them. Still, if we're going to successfully educate Black girls, we must have an honest discussion about racism and sexism.

Earlier, in the Herstory chapter, we offered classic statements and questions. Use those statements and questions as a springboard for this conversation. I would love to work with your staff to abolish racism and sexism in your school. For those who want to go one step further, read critical race feminist theory to get a fuller understanding of the problems.

Too many teachers still naively believe that they don't see race or color. They see children as children. They treat all children the same. (If you treat all children the same you will not allow for their differences in learning styles, attention span, energy levels, and much more.) The problems will persist as long as teachers remain in denial. I submit the following steps to help you remedy this problem:

1. Understand that you are in denial. You do see race. You do see color. You do see gender. You do not treat all children the same.
2. Admit that race, culture and gender are factors in the classroom.
3. *Understand* the race, culture and gender of your students.
4. *Appreciate* the race, culture and gender of your students.

If we are going to successfully educate African American girls, then teachers must not only be more honest with themselves and admit their views and feelings publicly about race, culture and gender of their students, but most important, they must take the time to examine their own prejudices and begin the learning process.

Time on Task

One of the most effective ways to increase proficiency in reading and math is to increase time on task. We must do a better job of managing the school day.

Researchers have found that many schools are losing fully one-third of the school day to student disengagement. Teachers and administrators are spending more time disciplining children than they are educating them. Students are allowed to text, listen to music, make comments on Facebook and Twitter, watch YouTube videos, send emails, and sleep in class. As these nonessential activities are eliminated, we can begin to increase time on task. Increasing time on task improves academic performance.

I'm reminded of the Native American Charter School in Oakland, California. Test scores rose from the 10th percentile to the 90th percentile when the time children spent going from class to class was virtually eliminated.[54] Instead, they decided to have *teachers* move from class to class. Some schools have chosen to implement block periods. Rather than students moving every 45 to 50 minutes, in a block period the class is now 90 to 100 minutes, thus reducing the movement of students by 50 percent. Some schools have moved some teachers closer together to reduce student time in transit. These are excellent strategies for educators who are serious about increasing time on task.

One of the major reasons for the success of the KIPP Schools, Urban Prep, Eagles, or many other schools is that they added one to two extra hours to the school day. I encourage schools to try and add a half-hour to an hour to increase time on task.

I realize that with union contracts, this is a highly sensitive issue. We have to be vigilant in looking for ways to improve academic performance without violating any union contracts.

Unfortunately, the agrarian economy that used to be in existence decades ago still dominates the summer months in parts of the country that have nothing whatsoever to do with farming. For some reason we are still closing schools three months during the summer as we did in the 1800s. If students are disengaged from learning for three months every summer for 12 years, that's 36 months—and this explains a great deal about the academic gap between Black and White students. We must keep African American children engaged during the summer months. We could redesign our school year, where rather than three consecutive months out of school, we have school for nine weeks, then three weeks out, nine weeks in, three weeks out. That's one possibility. Or ideally, we could increase the number of weeks that students are in school as is done in Germany and Japan.

If your school still sends students home for the three months of summer, then it's important to find creative ways to keep Black girls engaged—and that means more than just sending home a packet of worksheets in June and expecting them to be completed by the end of August. We need to use our partners—our churches, park districts, community organizations, and businesses—to provide activities for students so they can remain academically engaged during the summer. Internships, apprenticeships, work/study combinations, community gardening, and job shadowing are among the possibilities.

Suspensions/Expulsions

Twelve percent of Black girls are suspended and 8 percent expelled. Black girls are suspended or expelled four times as often as White girls. I strongly recommend only in-house school suspensions, but there's much more I want to say here.

- Only 20 percent of the teachers are making 80 percent of suspension/expulsion referrals. We need strong principals to monitor, and ideally remove, the 20 percent.
- Be fair. If White girls are not suspended or expelled for infractions of school policies, then Black girls shouldn't be either.
- Black girls should not be suspended or expelled because they violated the school uniform policy, used their mobile device, were loud, moved their neck, put their hands on their hips, or because the teacher simply did not like their attitude.
- Create a local school committee in charge of suspensions and expulsions. The committee should be made up of the principal, a Black female teacher or a teacher who loves Black female students, a Black female student, and a Black female parent. In order for a student to be suspended or expelled, there would have to be unanimous approval by the local school committee.
- I am an advocate of Restorative Practice. My version is the program Unity/Criticism/Unity (U/C/U). When needed, students start in a unity circle and offer compliments to each other. Second, they

offer any constructive criticisms and the defendant can respond. Last, the students determine the verdict and the punishment. We have found the students respect restorative justice more from their peer group and they will try to avoid U/C/U. We conclude the session in unity with more compliments and good news.

Designate a room in the school building for in-house suspensions and call it the "Tubman-Turner-Davis Room," named after Harriet Tubman, Mary Turner, and Angela Davis. The primary goal is to reduce the number of Black girls being suspended, but if a time-out is truly warranted, the student will first go to the Tubman-Turner-Davis Room. Not only will they work on class assignments there, they will watch movies such as *Dark Girl, Good Hair, Free Angela, Harriet Tubman, The Rosa Parks Story, Betty and Coretta, Akeelah and the Bee,* and *Winnie Mandela,* just to name a few.

Stock the Tubman-Turner-Davis Room with *Best Books for Girls* from African American Images as well as books written by the Black women writers listed earlier in this book. Put posters of African American women on the walls, including the "Phenomenal Woman" poster. Another poster will read:
1. Diploma
2. Degree
3. Career
4. Marriage
5. Baby

Have the girls write about the following topics:
- Are you a B or a Q (queen)?
- Do you have an attitude?
- Why do you fight?
- Are you a leader?
- Are you a bully?
- Are you a peace maker?
- Name five girls you don't like and why.
- Name five girls you like and why.
- Research and write about Harriet Tubman, Mary Turner, and Angela Davis.

Chapter Nine: Educational Solutions

I also encourage the staff in this room to monitor the students' Facebook and other social media comments. These are just a few of the activities and projects that will take place in the Tubman-Turner-Davis Room. Principals should have a mandatory in-service workshop to explain the various components of this in-house suspension room.

Monthly Convocation
The success of Spelman and Bennett, the only two colleges for African American women in the country, can be attributed in part to their convocations. Periodically, a motivational speaker is invited to inspire and encourage the students. The monthly convocation at your school should celebrate Black females and not become a gripe session. The topics should include more than fighting, attitude, loudness, boys, teen pregnancy, and STDs. We recommend the focus be on: goal setting, career development, leadership training, and how to recognize and resist racism, sexism and income inequality. The convocation should accentuate the beauty of Black females and promote unity.

BET has been involved in a program called *Black Girls Rock*. Not only is it an entertainment show on BET, it is an actual organization that offers a summer camp by the same name. I recommend that your school name the convocation Black Girls Rock. Have your girls involved in all aspects of the program.

Have your Black female students apply to participate in the summer camp. I'm excited about this excellent program because Black girls really rock!

Peer Mentoring
We all know about the harm that can be caused by negative peer pressure, but under your guidance, peer pressure can be transformed into peer inspiration, peer motivation, and peer encouragement. Peers can learn to encourage and model academic achievement for each other. Have fifth grade girls mentor third grade girls for two years. Have seventh grade girls mentor fifth grade girls for two years. Have 11th-grade girls mentor ninth-grade girls for two years. I believe we can raise test scores and reduce retention, suspensions, and the dropout rate with peer mentoring.

Adult Mentoring
Our girls need mentors, especially when only five percent of teachers are African American females. Ideally, there should

be one adult female mentor for every girl in your school. If that's not possible, then identify 20 of your more challenging girls and 20 Black female mentors to work with them for four consecutive years. Principals, ask each staff person to identify one Black female mentor. Reach out to the larger community, churches, businesses, and colleges to find mentors. Contact Black sororities, National CARES Mentoring Movement (Susan Taylor's program), Million Women Mentors, and the Boys and Girls Clubs. There are a wealth of resources available, if only schools would use them.

Rites of Passage
When does a girl become a woman? Our girls don't know. They don't know what's required. Some think having a boyfriend, having sex, or having a baby makes them a woman. Many girls think being a woman begins with the onset of menstruation. In African culture, girls are taken through a process called a rites of passage to usher them into womanhood. There's a clear understanding of the difference between being a girl and a woman, a boy and a man.

There are certain stages, requirements, and prerequisites that a girl must satisfy to earn the honor of being called a woman. We need to provide, either before, during, or after school, a rites of passage class. For more information read *Herstory: Black Female Rites of Passage* by Mary Lewis, *Sisters Helping Sisters* by Dr. Madeleine Wright, *Project Butterfly: Supporting Young Women and Girls of African Descent Through the Transitions of Life* by Niambi Jaha-Echols, *Black Girlhood Celebration* by Ruth Brown, and many more.

After the girls have taken the class, they will participate in a ceremony (it can be folded into Black Girls Rock). The purpose of the ceremony is to recognize their successful completion of the rites of passage program. The girls are bestowed the honor of being called a woman.

School Retention
Throughout this book, we have pointed out that a disproportionate number of Black girls are retained. Twenty-one percent is simply too high and unacceptable. In addition, the burden seems to be borne solely by the student. If the student failed, so did the school. Can you imagine a school retaining a girl and giving her the same teacher, curriculum, and pedagogy for the next

school year while expecting a different outcome? That borders on insanity.

We must abolish social promotions. As more and more strategies presented in this book are implemented, ideally fewer and fewer African American girls will be retained. However, for those girls who have not met the requirements of their grade level, I believe retention would be a far better option than social promotion. Students who are illiterate and do not know their multiplication tables in eighth or ninth grade are at risk of dropping out. We can't allow this to happen.

If a student must be retained, the school must bear 50 percent of the responsibility. Schools with a positive culture believe if the student has not learned, the teacher has not taught. Schools should do everything possible to ensure these students are brought up to grade level as quickly as possible. These students must receive the best teachers and SETCLAE. Pedagogy must become congruent with students' learning styles. Single gender cooperative learning groups will help these girls tremendously. Be relentless about increasing time on task.

Single Gender Classrooms and Schools

Use single gender cooperative learning as much as possible. In a class of 15 boys and 15 girls, there would be three groups of five boys and three groups of five girls. Black youth really benefit from cooperative learning groups.

Research shows that girls really benefit from a single gender experience when taking math and science classes.[55] Therefore, I recommend that every math and science class be taught within a single gender context.

I encourage you to visit a single gender school so you can see some of the exciting things taking place. I'm even more excited about the increase of single gender female STEM schools. Slowly but surely, we are bridging the STEM divide with single gender schools, classrooms, and cooperative learning groups. We can expect tremendous outcomes from single gender learning.

STEM

STEM primary. In the STEM chapter, I mentioned the excellent companies that are providing fantastic resources to help girls in the area of spatial intelligence. Every school should acquire the materials from GoldieBox, Roominate, and Sabotage at the Space Station. Also use Legos®, Rubik Cubes, maps, puzzles, and any toy that requires girls to take them apart and put them back together to improve spatial intelligence.

STEM intermediate. Every school should adopt the SciGirls curriculum to improve their girls' academic and STEM performance.

STEM high schools. The two gatekeeping subjects, algebra and biology, ideally should be taught by Black women teachers. If you cannot secure a Black woman teacher, then make sure to assign the *best* teacher. The best teachers not only have mastered the content and are certified in these subjects, but they like, respect, understand the culture, and love Black girls. They are fair. We want the best teachers for Black girls teaching algebra and biology. We also want to make chemistry, physics, geometry, trigonometry, and calculus available and mandatory for Black female students.

Drop Box

We want to hear what Black girls have to say. We want to empower them. We want their voices to be heard and respected. One way to do this is to install boxes throughout your school. Girls should be encouraged to write their comments and place them in the box. Comments will be reviewed by the same local school committee that reviews suspensions. These comments should be a springboard for discussions at staff meetings and in the teachers' lounge.

Reading

I believe the best way to improve reading scores for Black girls is to give them books that portray themselves. We must give them books they want to read. **We must give Black girls the opportunity to fall in love with reading.** Too many Black students only read irrelevant material in preparation to take a test. I recommend a monthly book club where Black girls can discuss the book they enjoyed reading. They should also write about this fantastic book. All the above will improve their vocabulary, comprehension, and writing skills. They must read books with characters that remind them of themselves. They must read about situations that reflect their lifestyle and culture. We must allow students to read at their own pace. We must be careful about asking a reluctant reader to read aloud. We must give phonics a larger role in our reading curriculum.

Towson University debate team made history in 2014 when Armeena Ruffin and Korey Johnson became the first African American female team to win the national championship.

Chapter Nine: Educational Solutions

Singapore Math

Memorizing is not understanding, but unfortunately in America, rote learning has been our approach to teaching math. This explains how students can perform math operations, but don't know which operation to use in a word problem. In America, we teach the skill first and then its application. In Singapore, the application or need is taught first, then the skill. Students memorize formulas without understanding. In contrast, the Singapore Math program teaches fewer concepts with greater depth and meaning.

Uncertified teachers should *not* be allowed to teach any subject. That should really be illegal. Can you imagine an uncertified doctor being allowed to perform surgery?

War Room

At least one staff person or a committee of volunteers should regularly identify students who are at greatest risk of dropping out and ending up on welfare or in the criminal justice system. Fifty-four percent of all women involved in penal institutions are Black females; that's one of every 19 Black women. In contrast, one of every 118 White women are involved.

The following is for all women, but Black females are 54 percent of those involved in the penal system:
- 113,000 are in prison.
- 93,000 are in jail.
- 712,000 are on probation.
- 103,000 are on parole.[56]

Educating Black Girls

Even more tragic, 64 percent of these women are mothers. Women get into serious trouble when they are caught in possession of a boyfriend's drugs, weapons, and stolen items. In fact, all of your students should read about Kemba Smith. A brilliant African American student at Hampton University, Kemba's college career was cut short when she became involved with a drug dealer. Because of mandatory drug sentencing laws, she faced 24 years and six months in prison. She ended up serving more than six years before being freed by President Bill Clinton. Black girls need to read Kemba's story to avoid what happened to her.

So your war room will be the place where rescue plans for Black girls at risk are made and implemented. These are your students who are performing poorly, have attendance below 90 percent, have been retained at least once, are scoring below proficient, and who have been suspended at least once. I encourage the staff in this room to monitor their students' social media comments. We can intercept fights by observing these comments. Monitor these students throughout the year to make sure they are making progress. Make these girls your priority. The goal is to save every Black girl this year.

What are you doing special for Black girls in your school? If you didn't know what to do, now you have several options that are research-based and will help improve outcomes. Review the above strategies and honestly assess how many you can implement in your school. What's preventing you from implementing as many as possible?

In the next chapter, we will look at post-high school options for Black girls. Not all girls are interested in college. We will look at their options after 12th grade.

Chapter Ten: Post-High School Options

In our society, it's either college or nothing. This chapter will look at options available for Black females after high school. If girls were bored with their K–12 (or less) experience, why would they want more of the same? They know college graduates who are unemployed and more than $50,000 in debt. College makes no sense to them.

First, let's look at what happens to the 40 percent of Black girls who drop out of high school. Do they return to school? Do they earn a GED? Do they enroll in a three-month, nine-month, one-year, two-year, or four-year college? Do they work? What is their hourly wage? Do they marry? Do they become pregnant? Do they end up on welfare? Do they become part of the criminal justice system?

We need to monitor and track the 40 percent of Black females who drop out of high school to ascertain what they're doing. How can we address their needs?

What happens to the 45 percent of Black females who graduate from high school, but either do not apply, cannot afford, are not accepted, or do not attend a two- to four-year college? Do they work? What is their hourly wage? Do they marry? Do they become pregnant? Do they become part of the welfare system? Do they become part of the criminal justice system?

Every school with Black female students should hold mandatory career development meetings in the last semester of the junior year and the first semester of the senior year. This will ensure that they understand their options for post-high school life.

Community colleges are some of the best institutions in America. They offer excellent majors that enable students to become employed immediately after graduation. If a student decides to pursue a four-year degree, going to a community college first to complete her general studies requirements is a cost-effective way of attending college. This shaves 50 percent off the final college bill.

Listed below are just a few popular majors at community colleges that provide employment almost immediately after graduation:
- Nursing Assistant
- Computer Information Systems
- Forensic Science

- Early Childhood Education
- Heating and Air Conditioning
- Refrigeration
- Architectural Drafting
- Graphic Design
- Automotive Technology
- Paralegal
- Real Estate
- Web Design
- Dental Assistant
- Physician Assistant
- Radiologist

I often ask Black girls if they know what they'll be doing when they're 30 years old. Our girls are not at risk because they're Black, have low income, and/or come from a single-parent home with a parent who lacks a degree. I believe they're at risk when they don't have any goals.

During my workshops, I often have students provide a different career for each letter of the alphabet, and they cannot use sports or entertainment. This assignment is always very challenging for students. Clearly, we have not properly prepared young people to understand the relationship between school and the larger economy. The mandatory career development meetings are an excellent way to help them understand. There are too many African American females who graduate from high school and wake up the next morning clueless about what their options are for the future.

What happens to the 54 percent of African American females who attend college, but don't graduate? Do they return to college? Do they transfer to another college? Are they employed? What is their hourly rate? Do they marry? Do they become pregnant? Do they end up on welfare? Do they become part of the criminal justice system?

What about the 46 percent of African American females who do graduate from college? Some college graduates are unemployed. Not only do we fail high school graduates by not providing career development for them when they're in high school, but many colleges do not prepare their graduates for life after college. Do our college graduates become employed? What is their hourly or annual wage? Do they marry? Do they become pregnant? Do they end up on welfare? Do they become part of the criminal justice system? What percent pursue graduate studies?

Chapter Ten: Post-High School Options

Internships

Any young woman would greatly benefit from working at least one internship. This is an excellent way to discover what type of work she would like to pursue and will help her gain practical experience in her chosen field. In Germany, high school graduates are encouraged to explore their career options through internships *before* entering college. They believe it's important to expose students to a wide array of career options. We, too, should expose our students to a wide array of internship experiences before college. This practical experience will help students decide on a major and make the course work more meaningful. I encourage your girls to enroll in the excellent program, Year Up.

Blue-Collar Jobs

Many Black women are tactile and kinesthetic learners, and blue-collar jobs can provide excellent work and wages for their specialized skills. The following are just a few white-/blue-collar jobs and what they pay.

Child care worker	$8/hour
Secretary	$10/hour
Bus or truck driver	$20/hour
Construction worker	$25/hour
Plumber, electrician, carpenter	$50/hour

If women's pay were equal to men's, poverty would be eradicated. How can a White male with a high school diploma earn more than a Black female with a college degree? We need to empower women, especially Black women. We need a society that is fair. Until child care workers, secretaries, nurses, and other female-dominated jobs are paid the same as males, then Black females need to pursue blue-collar trades, whether it's driving a truck or a bus, working in construction or a factory, or becoming a plumber, electrician, carpenter, or painter.

Business, Stock Market, Real Estate

In America, wealth is secured in primarily three areas: entrepreneurship, the stock market, and real estate. How many high schools in your city teach Black girls the principles of entrepreneurship? How many high schools in your city teach Black girls about the Dow Jones, NASDAQ, and S&P? How many high schools in your city teach Black girls the principles of real estate?

Business. There are more than 1.1 million Black female entrepreneurs. We need to teach Black girls how to start their own businesses. Before graduating from high school, Black girls should be required to come up with a business idea and write a business plan. They need to understand the principles of production, marketing, advertising, managing personnel, and accounting.

Ursula Burns, Chairman and CEO, Xerox

Chapter Ten: Post-High School Options

Oprah Winfrey, Black Female Billionaire and Media Tycoon

Risa Lavizzo-Mourey, President and CEO, Robert Wood Johnson Foundation

Debra Lee, President and CEO, BET

Cathy Hughes, President and CEO, TV One and Radio One

Chapter Ten: Post-High School Options

Linda Johnson Rice, CEO, Johnson Publishing Company

Rosalind Brewer, CEO, Sam's Club

Stock market. Schools should provide classes in investment principles. Every Black girl needs to know Rule 72. They need to know which stocks make up the Dow Jones and how the Dow Jones, NASDAQ, and S&P are different. Ask Black females to name the ten most popular products they purchase; Have them monitor the products on the stock exchanges.

Real estate. We need to teach Black girls how to acquire real estate. They should learn how to acquire property, rehab it, and then sell it for a profit. Teach them how to become a landlord, agent, broker, and investor. Black girls need to understand property management principles.

Sales

You will always have a job if you have sales skills. Sales is similar to public speaking. Many students are uncomfortable with public speaking, and many adults are uncomfortable with sales. We need to help our students become comfortable with public speaking and sales.

The best way to overcome your fear of selling is to first determine which products you like. Contact those companies and find ways that you can become part of their sales force.

Chapter Ten: Post-High School Options

Some of the best females in sales are Girl Scouts. Have you ever said no to a Girl Scout selling cookies? Clearly they believe in their mission, and they believe in their product. Once they are unleashed into the community, you can't stop them. Proof is their $700 million in annual sales.[57] The Girl Scouts is an excellent sales training ground for Black girls.

Few people who know how to sell are unemployed.

Few plumbers, electricians, carpenters, and painters are unemployed.

Few entrepreneurs and experts in real estate and the stock market are unemployed.

In closing, have you ever wondered why so many Black females are pursuing the military? Black females are 14 percent of the female population, but are 31 percent of the military.[58] In contrast, Black males are 16 percent. When unemployment is high and college is unaffordable, the military becomes a viable option. When you are poor and cannot afford college, military benefits are lucrative. Unfortunately, even the military has a problem with Black females and their natural hair.

Epilogue

In a hospital where one patient is on life support and another is in critical condition, doctors would not ignore the patient in critical condition. They would perform triage, allocating the appropriate resources to address the needs of both. This is how we should approach the challenges facing African American students; both girls and boys need our attention.

Black girls never should have been overlooked. While their challenges may not be as acute as those among Black boys, throughout this book you have seen that all is not well with Black girls.

- 82 percent of Black girls are below proficient in reading.
- 87 percent are below proficient in math.
- 21 percent are retained.
- 12 percent are suspended.
- 8 percent are expelled.
- 40 percent of Black females drop out.
- 2 percent of the doctors are Black females.

These figures are simply too high, unacceptable, cannot be overlooked, and need to be addressed. For too long, we have ignored Black girls and concentrated our efforts solely on African American males. This book is an attempt to bring attention to the plight of Black girls.

What do Black girls need more than anything else? I am reminded of Dr. Alisha Kiner, principal of Booker T. Washington High School in Memphis, Tennessee. Several years ago, with a graduation rate below 50 percent, her school became a recovery school. She was given the opportunity to pick and choose her staff, which every principal should be able to do. She only had one question for potential teachers: Do you love Black students?

The next year, the graduation rate soared to more than 80 percent. The last time I looked her students were still Black, had low income, came from single-parent homes, and had parents who lacked college degrees and were not involved in the girls' school progress. The only variable that changed was the focus on loving students. If there is one thing Black girls need, it's love.

Too many Black girls are in hostile environments where they are sent to the corner, removed from class, suspended, and expelled because the teacher did not like a student's hair texture or the scent of her moisturizer.

Too many Black girls are in schools where they read the work of Frederick Douglass, provided a brilliant analysis of the book, but were chastised and removed from the school.

Epilogue

Too many Black girls are criticized, degraded, called the N-word and B-word, not just by their peers, but by staff as well.

If there's one thing that Black girls need, it's love. Black girls need teachers who not only love them, but love their beautiful attitudes. Black girls need teachers to say, "Give me more attitude!" They need teachers to tell them that they like their attitude, they like who they are, the way they look, their hue, the texture of their hair, the way they walk and talk, their confidence and style. That's what Black girls need. They need educators who believe Black girls rock!

First Lady Michelle Obama was a brilliant high school student at a magnet school in Chicago. She was told by her counselor that she would never be admitted into Princeton. She graduated from Princeton and obtained a law degree from Harvard.

In closing, there's one last statistic I want to dissect because the numbers just don't add up. Black girls score 17.1 on the ACT, and Black boys score 16.8. The differential is only three-tenths, yet there are 2.3 million Black females in college, but only 1.4 million Black males.

Of the college degrees earned by African Americans, Black women earned:

- 68 percent of associate degrees
- 66 percent of bachelor's degrees
- 71 percent of master's degrees
- 65 percent of doctorate degrees

I'm trying to understand how scoring a mere three-tenths above Black males on the ACT has produced such wide disparities. How do you explain the tremendous success of young Black women at the collegiate level? I don't think we can attribute this success to their K–12 education. Scoring 17.1 on the ACT was the outcome of attending those schools. Yet despite the dismal performance of Black girls K–12, they are soaring at the collegiate level.

Dr. Venus Evans-Winters, in her excellent book, *Teaching Black Girls Resiliency in Urban Classrooms,* believes that resiliency is the primary protective success factor that enables them to excel despite their poor performance K–12. In my next book, *Raising Black Girls,* we will look at the factors outside of school—home, church, and community at large—that help develop strength and resiliency within Black girls. We will look at why they are so responsible, motivated, mature, organized, and able to meet deadlines. In *Raising Black Girls,* we will look at the dynamic in which some mothers raise their daughters and love their sons.

Notes

1. Michael Holzman, *Minority Students and Public Education* (Briarcliff Manor: Chelmsford Press, 2013); Trip Gabriel, "Proficiency of Black Students Is Found to Be Far Lower Than Expected," *New York Times,* November 9, 2010. http://www.nytimes.com/2010/11/09/education/09gap.html?_r=0; Catherine Gewertz, "NAEP [National Assessment of Educational Progress] Scores Inch Up in Math, Reading," *Education Week,* November 13, 2013. http://www.edweek.org/ew/articles/2013/11/13/12naep-2.h33.html

2. Monique Morris, *Black Stats* (New York: New Press, 2014), 16; Jane David, "What Research Says about Grade Retention," *Educational Leadership,* March 2008, 83-84. http://www.ascd.org/publications/educational-leadership/mar08/vol65/num06/Grade-Retention.aspx

3. *Black Stats,* 16.

4. Council of the Great City Schools, Washington, DC. http://www.cgcs.org

5. Caralee Adams, "Most Students Aren't Ready for College, ACT Data Show," *Hechinger Report,* August 21, 2013. http://www.hechinger report.org/content/most-students-arent-ready-for-college-act-data-show_12951/

6. *The Urgency of Now: The Schott 50 State Report on Public Education and Black Males* (Cambridge, MA: The Schott Foundation, 2012).

7. Marcia Greenberger, et al., *When Girls Don't Graduate, We All Fail* (Washington, DC: National Women's Law Center, 2007). When_girls_dont_graduate.pdf

8. Joy Heather Reskovits, "School Discipline Gap Explodes as 1 in 4 Black Students Suspended, Report Finds," *Huffington Post,* April 8, 2013. http://www.huffingtonpost.com/2013/04/08/school-discipline-gap

9. Nia-Malika Henderson, "Study: Black Girls Suspended at Higher Rates than Most Boys," *Washington Post,* March 21, 2014. http://www.washington post.com/blogs/she-the-people/wp/2014/03/21/study-black-girls-suspended-at-higher-rates-than-most-boys/

10. "African Americans by the Numbers," U.S. Census Bureau, July 1, 2012. www.infoplease.com/spot/bhmcensus1

11. Jimmy R. Ellis, "Examining the Low College Graduation Rates of Black Students," *Journal of Student Affairs,* 16, 2007, 29-34.

12. Ivory Toldson, "Cellblock vs. College," *Empower Magazine,* April 20, 2011. http://www.empowermagazine.com/cellblock-vs-college/

13. "Incarcerated Women," The Sentencing Project. http://www.sentencingproject.org/.../cc_incarcerated_women

14. Peggy Peck, "Teen Pregnancies on the Rise Again," ABC News. http://www.abcnewsgo.com/Health/reproductive

Notes

15. Linda C. Tillman, ed. *Sage Handbook of African American Education* (Thousand Oaks: Sage, 2009).

16. Patrick Bajari and Matthew E. Kahn, "Why Do Blacks Live in the Cities and Whites Live in the Suburbs?" Social Science Research Network, March 2001. SSRN-id263049.pdf

17. Civil Rights Data Collection: Data Snapshot (College and Career Readiness). Issue Brief No. 3, March 21, 2014, crdc-college-and-career-readiness-snapshot.pdf. www.2.ed.gov

18. Alicia Freese, "Education Funding Mechanism Needs Tweaking, Say Lawmakers and Governor," *Vermont Digger,* November 24, 2013. http://vtdigger.org/2013/11/24/education-funding-mechnism-needs-tweaking-say-lawmakers-governor/

19. Susan B. Neuman, *Changing the Odds for Children at Risk* (New York: Teacher's College Press, 2009), 106-112.

20. Kimberly Gedeon, "Only Two Percent of Scientists and Engineers Are Black Women despite Lucrative Careers in STEM," *Madame Noire,* November 19, 2013. http://www.madamenoire. com/324130/women-outnumber-men-stem-fields-underrepresented-others/

21. Zenitha Prince, "Study: Black Women Falling Behind in STEM Fields," *New Pittsburgh Courier,* December 1, 2013. http://newpittsburgh courieronline.com/2013/12/01/study-black-women-falling-behind-in-stem-fields/

22. Susan Goetz, *Science for Girls: Successful Classroom Strategies* (Lanham: Scarecrow, 2007), 15.

23. "Teachers of Mathematics and Science," *Science and Engineering Indicators 2012.* Arlington, VA: National Science Foundation, National Center for Science and Engineering Statistics (NCSES), January 2012. http://www.nsf.gov/statistics/seind12/c1/c1s3.htm

24. Goetz, 17.

25. Ruth Nicole Brown, *Black Girlhood Celebration: Toward a Hip-Hop Feminist Pedagogy* (New York: Lang, 2009), 19-30.

26. Paul E. Peterson, et al., *Globally Challenged: Are U.S. Students Ready to Compete?* Cambridge, MA: Harvard University, Program on Educational Policy and Governance. PEPG Report No.: 11-03, August 2011. PEPG11-03_GloballyChallenged.pdf

27. Carol Dweck, "Is Math a Gift? Beliefs That Put Females at Risk," in S. J. Ceci and W. Williams, eds., *Why Aren't More Women in Science? Top Researchers Debate the Evidence* (Washington, DC: American Psychological Association, 2006). http://www.stanford.edu/dept/.../cdweckmathgift.pdf

28. Jeffrey Howard, The Efficacy Institute. http://www. efficacy.org

29. Teacher Expectations and Student Achievement (TESA), Arlington (VA) Public Schools. http://www.apsva.us/1262

30. A. Wade Boykin, Brenda A. Allen, and Eric Alexander Hurley, "Study Finds That Black Youngsters Perform Better Academically in Different Types

of Learning Environments than Do Whites," *Journal of Blacks in Higher Education,* June 18, 2009. JBHE-on-CogInst-Ppr-wholepage-6_18_09.pdf

31. Goetz, 86.

32. Christopher Brennan, "U.S. Ballerina Faces Discrimination at Bolshoi Academy," *The Moscow Times,* November 19, 2013. http://www.themoscowtimes.com/news/article/us-ballerina-faces-discrimination-at-bolshoi-academy/489887.html

33. Cheryl Hurd, "Controversy Surrounds Lunch Menu at Concord High School," NBC Bay Area, February 7, 2014. http://www.nbcbayarea.com/local/Controversy-Surrounds-Lunch-Menu-at-Concord-High-School243841091.html

34. Charles Mudede, "My Daughter, Her Hair, and the Seattle School District," *The Stranger,* June 3, 2010. http://www.thestranger.com/seattle/my-daughter-her-hair-and-the-seattle-school-district/Content?oid= 4180400

35. The Wage Gap, by Gender and Race. Info Please. http://ipa/A0882775.html

36. Venus Evans-Winters and Jennifer Esposito, "Other People's Daughters: Critical Race Feminism and Black Girls' Education," *Educational Foundations,* 24 (1-2), Winter-Spring 2010, ERIC No. EJ885912.

37. "Title IX Myths and Facts," New York: Women's Sports Foundation, March 18, 2013. http://www.womenssports foundation.org/en/home/advocate/title-ix-and-issues/what-is-title-ix-myths-and-facts

38. The Battle for Gender Equity in Athletics in Elementary and Secondary Schools, Fact Sheet. Washington, DC: National Women's Law Center, January 30, 2012. http://www.nwlc.org/resource/battle-gender-equity-athletics-elementary-and-secondary-schools; Battle for Gender Equity in Athletics in Colleges and Universities, Fact Sheet. Washington, DC: National Women's Law Center, May 13, 2014. http://www.nwlc.org/resource/battle-gender-equity-athletics-colleges-and-universities

39. William C. Rhoden, "Black and White Women Far from Equal under Title IX," *New York Times,* June 10, 2012. http://www.nytimes.com/2012/06/11/sports/title-ix-has-not-given-black-female-athletes-equal-opportunity.html?pagewanted= all& r=0

40. Ibid.

41. Alan Mozes, "Hair Concerns May Discourage Exercise for Some Black Women," *Health Day, U.S. News and World Report,* December 17, 2013. http://health.usnews.com/health-news/news/articles/2012/12/17/hair-concerns-may-discourage-exercise-for-some-black-women

42. U.S. Office of Minority Health, Obesity Data/Statistics. Washington, DC: U. S. Department of Health and Human Services. http://minorityhealth.hhs.gov/

43. Battle for Gender Equity in Athletics in Elementary and Secondary Schools, Fact Sheet. Washington, DC: National Women's Law Center, January 30, 2012. http://www.nwlc.org/resource/battle-gender-equity-athletics-elementary-and-secondary-schools; Battle for Gender Equity in Athletics

Notes

in Colleges and Universities, Fact Sheet. Washington, DC: National Women's Law Center, May 13, 2014. http://www.nwlc.org/resource/battle-gender-equity-athletics-colleges-and-universities

44. Edward W. Morris, "'Ladies' or 'Loudies'? Perceptions and Experiences of Black Girls in Classrooms," *Youth & Society,* 38(4), June 2007, 490-515. doi: 10.1177/0044118X06296778

45. Data Snapshot: School Discipline – U.S. Department of Education, Office for Civil Rights, crdc-discipline-snapshot.pdf. www.2.ed.gov

46. Elijah Anderson, *Streetwise: Race, Class and Change in an Urban Community* (Chicago: University of Chicago Press, 1990).

47. Monique Morris, "Black Girls and School Discipline: What's Going On?" *Ebony Magazine,* April 2014. http://www.ebony.com/news-views/black-girls-and-school-discipline-whats-going-on-034#axzz33J0prDeh

48. Ibid.; Crystal Lewis, "Pushed Out of School, Black Girls Lose Huge Ground," *WE News,* March 24, 2010. http://womensenews.org/story/incarceration/140322/pushed-out-school-black-girls-lose-huge-ground#.U0rmYpUU_IU

49. Thomas S. Dee, "Teachers, Race, and Student Achievement in a Randomized Experiment," National Bureau of Economic Research, Working Paper No. 8432, August 2001. http://www.nber.org/papers/w8432

50. April Reese Sorrow, "Minority Teachers Reduce African-American Teen Pregnancy Rates," *Phys.org,* November 6, 2013. http://www.phys.org/news/2013-11-minority-teachers-african-american-teen-pregnancy.html

51. Marta D. Collier, "Changing the Face of Teaching: Preparing Educators for Diverse Settings," *Teacher Education Quarterly,* 29(1), Winter 2002, 49-59.

52. Cynthia Koptowski, "Why They Leave," *NEA Today Magazine,* Washington, DC: National Education Association, April 2008. http://www.nea.org/home/12630.htm

53. Joy Williams, *Unspoken Realities: White Female Teachers Discuss Race, Students and Achievement in the Context of Teaching in a Majority Black Elementary School* (Ann Arbor: ProQuest, 2008).

54. Ben Chavis, *Crazy Like a Fox: One Principal's Triumph in the Inner City* (New York: Penguin, 2009), 28.

55. "Research Spotlight on Single-Gender Education," Teaching Strategies, NEA. http://www.nea.org/tools/17061.html

56. "Incarcerated Women," The Sentencing Project.

57. Thomas McEnery and Gus Lubin, "How the Girl Scouts Built Their $700 Million Cookie Empire," NBC News, 2012. http://www.nbcnews.com/id/42270952/ns/business-small_business/t/how-girl-scouts-built-their-million-cookie-empire/#.U4oNssU.IU

58. James Dao, "Black Women Enlisting at Higher Rates in U.S. Military," *New York Times,* December 22, 2011. http://www.nytimes.com/2011/12/23/us/black-women-enlist-at-higher-rates-in-us-military.html